# DRIVE

# DRIVE

## SCRAPING BY IN UBER'S AMERICA, ONE RIDE AT A TIME

## JONATHAN RIGSBY

BEACON PRESS • BOSTON

BEACON PRESS
Boston, Massachusetts
www.beacon.org

Beacon Press books
are published under the auspices of
the Unitarian Universalist Association of Congregations.

"The Chemical Worker's Song": Lyrics graciously
provided by the estate of Ron Angel.

27  26  25  24      8  7  6  5  4  3  2  1

This book is printed on acid-free paper that meets the uncoated paper
ANSI/NISO specifications for permanence as revised in 1992.

Text design and composition by Kim Arney

*Library of Congress Cataloging-in-Publication Data is available for this title.*
ISBN: 978-0-8070-0793-8; e-book: 978-0-8070-0792-1; audiobook:
978-0-8070-3534-4

*For my little bear.*

■ ■ ■ ■ ■ ■

*And it's go, boys, go!*
*They'll time your every breath.*
*And every day you're in this place,*
*You're two days nearer death.*

*But you go.*

—RON ANGEL,
"The Chemical Worker's Song"

# CONTENTS

# INTRODUCTION

WHEN I WAS A TEENAGER, I HAD A TELEVISION IN MY BEDROOM THAT I INHERITED from my brother's room after he moved out. My parents gave it to me with the promise that I wouldn't let it distract me from my schoolwork. At night, long after my parents went to sleep, I would stay up and do homework or play video games on my computer with the TV on in the background. I mostly put it on as a companion. With very few friends and a limited social life, I felt less alone hearing the voices of other people in the background.

In those days, there was a show called *Taxicab Confessions* that came on just after Dennis Miller finished his political talk show. The show's premise was simple: a taxi driver in some city (usually Las Vegas) would pick people up, and hidden cameras would record them as they talked about their most private and intimate secrets.

As a kid, I was fascinated by the things that people would admit to a total stranger. There were wild discussions of drug use, sexual escapades, and stories of such immense sadness that I found them difficult to believe. Even though the show included a disclaimer at the start that the people involved had signed a waiver to release the footage, I knew that the show *had* to be scripted. There was no way people would admit the types of things they said to those cab drivers. I had always believed that things would just work out. As long as I worked hard, my natural intelligence would carry me through. My parents told me I was smart and capable; surely others would see the same in me, and the world would be my oyster. It wasn't until a drunk lobbyist berated me for missing the turn onto his street that I realized how wrong I had been.

Between bouts of yelling into his phone that the senator had better change the bill if he wanted to see another dime from the lobbyist's clients, he told me in no uncertain terms that my failure to spot a street sign in the dark of an unfamiliar neighborhood was the result of my faulty upbringing and mentally deficient parents. As he got out, I told him to have a nice night. He told me to go fuck myself.

If you've never worked in a service industry, you may think you'd never put up with being treated that way, but all across America, it's the daily reality of servers and cashiers and anyone who lives paycheck to paycheck (which is more people than you think). When you are desperate, truly desperate, you'll swallow your pride if it means you don't have to be hungry anymore.

There's an ugly truth that hides in the gaudy background of the American dream: you can do everything right and still fail.

∎  ∎  ∎

I was privileged enough to attend a world-class university after high school. My parents paid for my undergraduate degree, and I assumed meaningful work would automatically follow. I drifted from my home in Alabama to Washington, DC, then back to my hometown of Montgomery. I worked in a local video game store while saving money and applying to graduate school, flush with dreams of saving the world with a degree in international relations. After two rounds of applications, I was accepted to another university in Chicago.

I reunited with my girlfriend from college as we moved to the Windy City together. For the next two years, I studied hard. My dream job was just around the corner. Any day now, I thought, it would all work out. Job after job fell through, and by the time I graduated, I had nothing lined up. My girlfriend, now my fiancée, had been accepted to a graduate program in Tallahassee, and we moved to Florida so she could go to school. I worked part-time at another local video game store before landing a steady, full-time job working for the State of Florida's child welfare program, the Department of Children and Families (DCF). Finally, I felt, I could find my feet. My fiancée and I were going to make a home.

It was an unusual position, that first real job. The agency needed a DCF person to sit inside the headquarters of the state police and help coordinate the response when children in foster care went missing. A system in Florida filed dozens of reports each day for children who ran away from foster care, and any time they weren't quickly located, a case would be opened with the state missing persons clearinghouse.

For the next three years, I spent my days diligently reading through the case files of abused and neglected children, searching for information that might be helpful in locating them when they went missing. In each case, I read through the allegations and notes from case workers, absorbing a world of abuse, abandonment, and neglect. I learned to recognize the signs that a foster child was involved in sex trafficking and notified care agencies when children were being victimized. It was, by turns, brutal and rewarding.

The sheer darkness of the work took a toll on me mentally, and I would sometimes find myself crying in my car after a particularly disturbing case came up. Constantly reading about child abuse was difficult, but it became unbearable when my newly married wife told me she was pregnant. In every file, every broken bone and hollow-eyed victim statement, I saw my own child and wondered how such things were possible.

As I was isolated from the main office at DCF, my work went largely unnoticed, but within the law enforcement world, my analytical abilities were being discussed behind closed doors. I was quietly encouraged to apply for a position as an intelligence analyst in the counter-terrorism section, and after a series of interviews, the job was mine. Things slowly began to fall into place. I was moving into a career that I was proud of, and my wife and I were experiencing the sleep-deprived joy of our first child.

.  .  .

On the other side of the country, a group of software engineers were perfecting a new way of working. Flush with millions in venture capital, they had launched an app that would allow users to call a private car to drive them to their destination. They hired computational neuroscientists, nuclear physicists, and an army of programmers to design a system that allowed any person to sign up and use their personal vehicle as a taxi. With infinite money and a brain trust dedicated to finding ways to exploit the reward pathways of the human brain, the system was designed to shift costs onto the vulnerable individuals who just needed a little bit of extra money to make ends meet.

By the time my life fell apart and I signed up to become a ride-share driver, the entire ecosystem was already established. Waves of drivers were signing up every week to wear out their personal vehicles driving strangers back and forth across town for meager earnings. In Uber's offices, executives reveled in the endless praise of the media, who lauded them for "disrupting" the stagnant taxi industry. Across the country, an army of drivers was chasing a phantom dream of being one's own boss, shuttling people to and fro over long nights and early mornings while Uber's executives appeared on magazine covers.

The nature of work in America was changing, transforming so rapidly that traditional structures could barely react to the rapid decay of the American lifestyle. In the 1990s, futurists had dreamed of a world where technology would make every person's life safer, easier, and more rewarding. Far from a safety net, technology re-invented the sweatshop model of piecemeal work that had once been abolished in America by pesky regulations like the minimum wage, and millions fell into the system because traditional work no longer paid the bills. The new method had its own name, one that soon became ubiquitous: the gig economy. People were now freed to work when and where they wanted. So long as they chose to forego decent earnings and workplace safety, the sky was the limit.

By placing all of the earning responsibility on the drivers, Uber had perfected a passive model of wealth extraction: do none of the *actual* work and skim a percentage of the money earned by drivers for the company. That the system was not yet profitable was a problem to be handled in the future. As long as customers preferred a stranger's barely regulated vehicle to a taxicab, ride-share would grow like a weed, and the model it presented would eventually be adapted to everything from food delivery to grocery shopping. The technology created a world of digital servants that lived just out of sight but could be conjured into existence to provide consumers with any number of services. At the tap of a screen, your own personal genie would bring you your heart's desire. Just don't think too hard about whether the genie has to sleep in their car at night.

.   .   .

I spent many hours in my car mulling over the events that led to my state of precarity, but even if I was isolated from friends and family, I wasn't alone. Over thousands of rides, passengers listened to me just as I listened to them. In ride after ride, I shared myself with total strangers, and they in return, revealed their fears, hopes, and secrets to me. Their lives were heartbreaking, touching, surprising, and even humorous in equal measure.

I struggled with poverty. I raged at the universe for its indifference to my suffering. I despaired that things would never be different. Then I tapped on my phone and picked up another ride. Eventually, I found a way through, but not before having to relearn everything I thought I had known about what matters in life. What you're about to read is the story of one father, three years, and more than eight thousand rides.

This is a story about how I rebuilt my life from behind the wheel of a car. It's a story about letting go of my dreams and learning to live with reality, about focusing on the things in life that really matter: family, love, and happiness. But this isn't just my story. It's a story that is being repeated across the United States countless times every day. It's the story of immigrants being taken advantage of and lied to about opportunities, of poor people being forced to compete against each other for scarce rewards, of desperate people doing desperate things just to survive. It's the story of digital America.

Are you ready?

Buckle up.

# CHAPTER 1

I GAVE MY FIRST UBER RIDE ON THANKSGIVING IN 2016. THERE WASN'T ANY grand symbolism behind this choice. I'd signed up to be a driver two weeks before, but Thursday was the first day I'd worked up the nerve to log on to the app and give it a try. I had serious questions about whether the ads touting the money I could make were little more than hot air. I needed a steady way to make money during odd hours, and Uber felt like a good solution. If it didn't work, I could always find something else.

Signing up had been the easy part. I'd sent in a picture of my driver's license and taken my car to a mechanic for a cursory vehicle inspection that mostly involved getting a form signed. There was some sort of background check conducted behind the scenes—not that I was worried; my day job probably had higher requirements. After that, I was cleared to start driving.

I sat in my car and stared at the app, unsure about how it worked. There had been some brief training videos that explained the idea, how to accept a ride and end it once I had dropped the passenger off or how often I would get paid, but all sorts of questions remained about the exact process. I remained deeply unsure that this would work, that I could make enough money to pay my bills by driving strangers around town in my free time. The whole

thing felt like a trick. Drive around and make money? It sounded
a little too good to be true, but at this point, I was committed to
at least try. I took a deep breath and tapped the big blue button
on the screen marked "GO."

A musical chime sounded, and the bottom of the screen
blinked with a different word: "ONLINE." I waited breathlessly
for a few minutes, expecting something to happen immediately.
Ten minutes later, I was still sitting in my parking space. Was
I supposed to start driving around? Should I stay in one place?
There was no one to ask and no answers to be had. Confusion
began to set in. Was I doing something wrong? I checked the
settings screen but could find nothing that seemed to apply. I listened to the radio for a few minutes and idly wondered if I should
go back inside and get a book. Maybe this wasn't going to work.

The app dinged, and I fumbled with the phone I had stuck to
my dashboard with a Velcro strip, a thrifty solution I'd come up
with when I couldn't afford one of the magnetic phone mounts
that Uber recommended. I accepted the ride without even seeing
where I was going. For the next few minutes, I struggled to deci-
pher exactly where my passenger was before pulling up in front of
the freshman dorms at Florida State University. A lone student
walked out, dragging a rolling suitcase. I helped him load it into
the back before swiping the app to start the ride.

*You can do this*, I told myself as the destination appeared on my
phone. I took a deep breath and one more glance at the stranger
in my backseat as I shifted into gear. As we set off for the airport,
I tried to make small talk, only to discover that the young man
spoke minimal English. The on-screen navigation was tiny and
difficult to read while talking and driving, and I eventually shut
up and focused on the car, ignoring the awkward silence that I

had created. The young man alternated between looking out the window and down at his phone.

I dropped him off in front of the terminal and swiped the app again, ending the ride. A small message popped up to announce my earnings: $7, enough for a cheap fast-food meal if I wanted to quit. I pulled out of the terminal and headed back into town to look for another ride. *Not that hard*, I thought.

I had barely made it back into town that first Thanksgiving Thursday before my phone dinged again. Still fumbling, I looked at the screen while trying not to swerve off the road. It showed a location, a name, and an estimate of how many minutes away I was from the pickup point. I tapped the screen to accept and started toward my next passenger. I arrived ten minutes later at a house in the suburbs where a large group of family members were hugging and saying their goodbyes.

As I pulled up to the curb, a preppy young couple that looked like they belonged at an Easter garden party broke off from the group, smiling and waving as they walked toward me. The man got into the car first, untying a sweater from around his shoulders and dropping it into his lap. His wife climbed in behind him and told him to scoot over.

"Jesus Christ, I'm glad that's over," the husband said before I could say hello. He buckled his seatbelt as his wife shot him a dirty look. "What? I hate your family." I put aside my greeting and focused on the app as it directed me to a nearby hotel. The young couple spent the entire ride arguing. I sat in uncomfortable silence.

Even before I dropped them off, my phone chimed again with another ride. I had assumed that Thanksgiving would be a quiet day, perfect for learning how being a driver worked. I was mistaken. What followed was a steady stream of rides from people who had come into town to visit family. While I don't associate Thanksgiving with heavy drinking, ride after ride told me how they had to throw a few back to put up with a certain uncle or tolerate listening to their grandfather's political rants. Everyone had somewhere to go or someone to get away from.

In the few gaps between rides, I was unsure of what to do with myself. Sometimes I kept moving, trying to head back toward the suburbs that I assumed were full of people wanting rides. Sometimes I pulled into a parking lot and looked at the news on my phone. I began to think that I really ought to have brought that book.

Before logging on that first day, I'd asked a local driver's group on Facebook for beginner's advice. While most of the replies were sarcastic, one stuck with me. A middle-aged woman told me to make sure to be friendly. "Try to figure out the right amount to talk," she wrote. "You want to make conversation, but also learn when to shut up. So talk . . . but not too much." It wasn't much to go on, but her profile picture showed her behind the wheel of her car. I figured she had to know what she was talking about. With her advice in mind, I pushed myself to make small talk with total strangers. A few hours of steady rides later, I had earned $50. Proud of myself, I drove home and made myself a grilled cheese sandwich with a stiff drink on the side.

The next day, I turned the app back on and waited for my first ping. So far, the best strategy seemed to be choosing a side of town and driving about aimlessly while I waited. With Black Friday sales in the shops, business was steady as I shuttled people back and forth from homes to stores and vice versa. Gone were the people complaining about their drunk uncles, replaced by people frenzied with consumer spending, even those who couldn't afford their own car.

Amid the shoppers with their bags of clothes and small electronics were more unusual rides, including a man with a 55-inch television. That the man with the TV did not have a way to transport this electronic monstrosity home was clearly an afterthought. As I pulled up outside the store, he flagged me down.

"Thank God you've got a big car," he said as I opened the back hatch of my SUV. He told me I was the third driver he'd called. The first two had shown up and driven off after determining they had no way to fit the box inside of their cars and had no interest in tying it to the roofs. As we lifted it into the back, I marveled at what I was enabling. This man who had taken the bus to Walmart clearly had no plan at all for his ill-conceived shopping trip.

I couldn't help but wonder what thought process had led him to this decision. Surely this was no impulse purchase. Had he planned on using Uber to get it home all along, or was I a last-ditch decision? As he told me about looking forward to setting it up in his apartment, I decided that my job wasn't to pass judgment on this man. My job was to drive the car.

I helped him carry the box to the second floor of his apartment complex, and he thanked me for my help.

"I couldn't have done it without you, brother," he said. "I'll make sure to tip you on the app." As I backed out of my parking space, it occurred to me that what he had just promised was impossible. There was no tipping integrated into the Uber app at this point, and it would not arrive for several more years. I shrugged, accepted the grace of his intention, and tapped the

screen for a ride at a nearby shopping mall. I worked until night-
fall before heading home to find a few brief moments of rest.

.  .  .

My decision to become a rideshare driver was driven by necessity,
not by desire. After my marriage ended, my expenses exceeded
my income by hundreds of dollars each month. If I was going to
survive, I had to find a way to earn that money. Because I still
had my day job with the state, I didn't qualify for any sort of
assistance with food or rent. Florida is notoriously stingy with
welfare benefits, and there was no allowance made for people
who were earning money but didn't get to keep it. Convinced
that I had disappointed everyone who cared about me, I couldn't
stomach the idea of asking my parents for help. They had done so
much for me, and here I was, starting over with nothing. My few
remaining friends lived in other states, and while I was grateful
for their moral and emotional support, they couldn't help me out
of my situation. I was alone.

Initially, I had tried to work a second job in retail. For months,
I worked the register of a video game store in the local mall, coming home to eat ramen noodles and grilled cheese sandwiches.
With most of my money taken up with rent, alimony, and child
support, I spent my nights replaying old video games and drinking
heavily. Miserable, lonely, and seeing no end in sight, I knew I
had to change something. Sharing custody of my son with my
now ex-wife meant that I had to try to schedule work at the
store around my day job and a toddler. It was stressful, hectic,
and complicated.

The biggest impediment was time itself. On days with my son,
I couldn't work until he was asleep in his bed at the house, and

no employer was going to want someone who could only work late nights and alternating weekend days. That the game store in the mall was accommodating me was due mostly to the mercy of the store manager. When I'd first moved to Tallahassee, I'd given him months of steady work before leaving on good terms for my job in the foster care system. I had been good for him, and he did me a favor by taking me back on. It wasn't a long-term solution. The hours he gave me were crowding out other employees that had been there longer, and I knew it.

I was living paycheck to paycheck on a razor-thin margin, ending every month with just a few dollars to spare. One car accident, blown tire, or major illness and I'd have been bankrupt. Even a co-pay to see a doctor would have been a major sacrifice, and I knew that I'd never be able to live long-term on a grocery budget of $40 a week. Birthday or Christmas presents for my son were impossible. I had to find something better than manning a register at the mall for just over minimum wage.

I explored all sorts of options for jobs, trying to find steady work like research or content writing. I investigated tutoring or writing term papers for unscrupulous students, but most options couldn't provide me with the hours or the income I needed. Everywhere I looked, I could find a few hours of high-paying work or lots of hours of low-paying work that wouldn't accommodate my schedule, but not both. As I scrolled and scrolled through job listings, I kept seeing advertisements to drive for Uber.

Before this, I had thought of a rideshare app as a curiosity, the sort of thing that only existed in big cities and was mostly experimental. Who was going to call some stranger and get in their car? I'd read articles that rideshare drivers were strapping pink moustaches to the front of their vehicles in San Francisco and taking people around town, but what would it look like in Florida? I had a suspicion that I could do pretty well in a college town. The advertisements for Uber all mentioned "being your own boss," and while I had no illusions that I was going to be running some sort of business, being able to work anytime I wanted was attractive.

I sat down and made a list of the pros and cons. Pro: I could choose my own hours to work. Cons: I was risking getting hurt in a car accident and I'd spend more money on gas, which would wreck my budget if I couldn't make it work. I knew that working as a rideshare driver would beat up my vehicle, leave me sitting down for long periods in my car, and inevitably end with someone puking in my backseat. I tried not to think about phrases like "deep vein thrombosis" and whether my life insurance policy would be enough for my son, Alex, to go to college.

What I actually needed was not another job but to take a break, a chance to breathe. I was spending every waking moment working, parenting, or worrying about how I would get through the week. I didn't need to do more; I needed to do less, to simplify my life. My workload was draining my ability to do anything well, but the only solution was to make more money. I was trapped, and my only way forward was to keep going and hope that things would get better before I collapsed.

My debt situation wasn't sustainable. I had nearly $10,000 in credit card debt racked up, not to mention hefty student loans from my graduate degree. Theoretically, I would be able to pay off the credit cards over time, but that assumed that nothing would ever go wrong. I had no savings or emergency fund. If there had been an emergency, my only solution would have been to choose which bill or expense to stop paying temporarily. I was already cutting back on my expenses. The ultimate nightmare was a vehicle breakdown or car accident, something that would take me off the road for an extended period. For that, there would be no solution.

In the end, the lone prospect of getting to choose my own work hours was too attractive. If it didn't work out, I didn't have to do it long-term, and there was a $200 bonus for signing up as a new driver once I'd done a certain number of rides. People wouldn't be driving for Uber if they couldn't make the numbers work, right?

# CHAPTER 2

"WHAT BROUGHT YOU TO TALLAHASSEE?"

The question caught me off guard. It was only my second day driving, and I wasn't prepared to deal with such a personal question from the older woman in my backseat. I struggled to find the right words to answer, eventually settling on a version of the truth: my fiancée had gotten into Florida State University for graduate school, and I'd moved to support her and be closer to my family in Alabama. It seemed like a good answer, but it merely opened the door for the obvious next question.

"Are you married now?"

I froze, feeling all the hot shame of the divorce welling up inside me. All the arguing and tears and marriage counseling that had amounted to nothing burned as a hot lump in my chest. I kept my voice neutral as I told her that we'd gotten divorced a few months ago.

"Oh . . . I'm sorry," she muttered. I finished the ride in silence and dropped her off as I tried to process what had just happened. In the few rides I'd given since signing up, I had found joy in being anonymous. When I was a stranger, I was a blank slate, free of the stigma I carried inside of me. Being asked (even in idle curiosity) about Marie dredged up months of emotional turmoil. I didn't want to lie, but the truth was still painful to acknowledge.

The year preceding this moment had been a whirlwind. My wife, Marie, and I bought a house, started arguing, and went to marriage counseling. Our two-year old son, Alex, was displaying aggressive behaviors at daycare, misbehaving and biting other children. At the office, I was capable and creative, writing intelligence reports about people on the federal terrorism watchlist that had a connection to Florida. My performance evaluations were glowing, and I was considered the go-to person for special projects or deep dives on particularly dangerous subjects. At home, my life was stressful, and I had an omnipresent feeling that I had failed as a husband in a way that couldn't be fixed. By the time she handed me the divorce papers, I was numb.

Marie had written the divorce agreement herself. I read through it twice, did some math, and agreed within days. With no money to hire a lawyer, I had to navigate the legal system by myself and guess at what was fair. Alleged criminals are guaranteed legal assistance as their cases move through the courts, but there's nothing like that for family or divorce court. As long as you stand in front of the judge and say you're fine with the divorce and custody agreements, courts aren't going to waste time asking you if you've sought an outside perspective. People told me to fight back, but I didn't have the emotional strength. Broken and exhausted, I signed what was put in front of me with little resistance.

I would retain 50 percent ownership of the house and pay half the mortgage, plus I would pay an additional amount each month for maintenance and repairs. Florida doesn't have "custody" per se, opting instead for a system of parental responsibility and time-sharing, but Alex would live and grow up in the house Marie and I bought together, just like we had planned. I would be allowed to visit a few days a week and one day every weekend, paying child support to make sure he had everything he needed. It was as close to a fifty-fifty split as we could manage. We would revisit that schedule in a year once I had the opportunity to get settled.

The first night after I finished moving into my postdivorce apartment, a dusty one-bedroom in a bad part of town with a half-size stove and a window AC unit, I locked the door and cried on the floor. My few possessions were a car, a couch, some odds and ends from the old kitchen, and a mattress for the floor.

■ ■ ■

After the first time someone asked me how I ended up in Tallahassee, I pulled into a gas station and took a break to collect myself. Needing to keep my energy (and my personality) up, I filled the biggest cup the gas station had with a mixture of diet soda and a cheap energy drink. The mixture tasted like lemon-lime battery acid, but it would keep me perky. I'd been so focused on the fine details of driving that I'd overlooked what would turn out to be the most significant part of the work: the people. Every time I logged on to drive, there would be an entire city of people who wanted to grill me about every detail of my life. Where was I from? Was I a student? Was this my only job? The man behind the wheel was the subject either of intense interest or benign neglect.

I understood their curiosity. At least in Tallahassee, rideshare was a novel experience in 2016. In a city of mostly government workers, healthcare professionals, and college students, rideshare apps like Uber had been slow to catch on outside of the college crowd. The prospect of getting to have a one-time encounter with an interesting stranger excited people; since they'd probably never see me again, there was no reason to hold back. If every rider was going to grill me about my personal life, I was going to have to lock my personal traumas in a box while I worked.

In a way, my previous work in the foster care system had prepared me for doing this. When you spend all day reading about child abuse, you're forced to develop a mental resiliency, a way of walling off your emotions from the work. When I first started the job, I'd spent my days listening to music before discovering the hard way that hearing the same song on the radio later could trigger flashbacks to particularly ugly details in a case file. I'd been forced to separate my emotions from the work, focusing on pushing through the files. It didn't matter how I felt about the details of a particular case. The work had to be done.

The same logic applied to my current circumstances. The key to survival was to keep moving. Passengers were going to ask me about myself, and I was going to have to answer their questions. It didn't matter if I was hungry or tired or depressed; the answers would have to be given with a smile. I was working because I needed to survive, and my feelings about my circumstances would have to wait at home while I was driving. Alex needed his father, and if I had to walk through fire to make sure he could fall asleep in his childhood home, I would do it.

The divorce had not been easy on him. Amid the chaos of my moving out, Marie and I had tried to keep everything as normal as possible. I often wondered if this had been a mistake. In his world, his father had been a constant presence, a reassuring source of love and safety until, one day, I was gone. I became a visitor, neither there in the mornings when he woke up nor present to tuck him into bed on most nights.

I agonized at what I knew I had lost. On the morning of Thanksgiving, Marie had invited me to the house for a small Thanksgiving meal. It meant so much to me to laugh and play with him, to see the one piece of family I had in Tallahassee on my favorite holiday. He had cried when I left, not understanding why I couldn't stay. I thought of the holidays that I would miss, the moments that I would never see. A part of me worried that he would never forgive me for my failure to keep things together. I consoled myself with my devotion. Yes, I had failed as a husband, but I would not fail my son.

On the weekend day I had with Alex, we stacked blocks and played peekaboo, spending most of the day in the small playroom in the back of the house where we could read books and race toy cars. Normally, I would bathe him and put him to bed before returning to my small apartment by the train tracks. Now though, I didn't have to go home. If I was angry or lonely or depressed, I could stick my phone to the dashboard and channel my frustrations into something productive. With every ride, I got a little bit closer to the things I wanted. A Christmas present for Alex. A pair of shoes that didn't have holes in the bottom. Maybe even a trip to the grocery store where I could indulge in something besides bare necessities. Every ping on the screen whispered to me the promise of a better life.

With Alex tucked into bed that first weekend, I said goodbye to Marie and climbed back into my car, anxious to see what the night would hold. After an entire day spent in the company of a very active toddler, I probably could have used a shower, but that would have eaten into my driving time. I logged on and turned out of the starter home community where Marie and I were supposed to have built our future together. The neighborhood had been zoned for some of the city's better schools, and even if it wasn't in the wealthiest area, there were certainly wealthy neighborhoods nearby. I hadn't seen any rides from this area yet, so I pulled into the parking lot of the local Costco and waited.

A few minutes later, I pulled into the driveway of a large house with a manicured lawn. An older couple walked out, on their way to a fancy restaurant. They thanked me for picking them up and told me that getting a ride on this side of town often took a long time. They buckled up and chatted with each other during the trip, ignoring me.

I dropped them off and thought about my location. I had gone from the edge of town to the center of the city in just a few minutes. Tallahassee isn't small, but it certainly isn't large. If I wasn't finding rides in one area, I could cross to the other side of town in twenty minutes. I had to hope that there would be enough business in the city to keep me busy, and so far, it had been steady. I just had to put in the time.

A ping from a local bar interrupted my thoughts, telling me that David was awaiting a ride. A young man, extremely drunk and in need of a ride home, climbed into the back. The questions started immediately, but this time, they took a different tack.

"How long have you been doing this?" David asked. I told him that it was only my third day, and this was my first nighttime shift. He laughed.

"I've been driving for a couple years. Nights and weekends are where all the money is. If you haven't met the college kids yet, you'll see."

This piqued my curiosity. I knew that Florida State University had a reputation as a hard-partying, heavy-drinking school, but I didn't have a point of reference for what that would actually

mean. The only people I'd seen were the locals, and despite living in the city for five years, I'd never encountered the college
nightlife. At thirty-one, I was too old to be dancing in clubs with
a bunch of kids.

David's voice brought me out of my reverie as we passed
through the empty streets on the way to his apartment. He told
me that my car was really clean. I asked if he had any tips for a
new driver. What followed was a series of vaguely useful tidbits
about gas stations with free vacuums and what fast-food place
had the cleanest bathrooms (Jimmy John's, if you're wondering).

"No," I interrupted, "I mean for the college kids."

"Oh," he said. "You'll have to figure that out for yourself."

After he left, I took another ride from a nearby shopping
mall. Outside, an exhausted retail worker waited to go home. She
thanked me for picking her up and told me she had just finished
working a double shift. Hungry and tired, she asked if we could
swing through a drive-thru to get something to eat. No problem,
I said. We pulled away.

"So," she said, "what brought you to Tallahassee?"

. . .

That first weekend driving was a false introduction to what was
to come. With most of the students gone for the Thanksgiving
holiday, nearly all my rides were from locals and adults who had
come to town to visit family. As the week began, I quickly learned
that my experience thus far had been the exception, not the rule.

I had earned a decent income in the first few days, but my
ignorance about where and how to make money cost me dearly.
All the hours on the road had burned a lot of gas, reducing my
earnings—$10 in my pocket quickly became $5 when there were

too many miles between pickups. As the hours ticked away at the
office on Monday, I wondered what I would see when I logged
on to the app.

I whittled away the hours doing some quick math. To make
up for the extra gas I was going to have to buy and still cover my
bills, I needed to make about $1,000 more in my car than what
I was making at the office each month. That came out to $250
a week, which I decided to divide up into a schedule of driving
Monday, Wednesday, Friday, and whatever weekend day I had to
myself. If I needed more, I could work at night after putting Alex
to bed. The hours would be long, but at least I was choosing them.

I created a separation in my mind between my day job and
what I was doing on the app. My life in the office, that was real
work. The extra money that I scraped together from Uber, that
was just driving. It wasn't a second job, just a little extra that I
needed to supplement my income. I had a good career, but my
financial situation necessitated that I had to come up with a little
more. I wasn't yet able to see that all of it was work, labor that
deserved fair compensation.

My financial situation was difficult, and the past few months
had forced me to adjust my expectations. Poverty was entirely
new to me. My struggles had to be taken one at a time, a thousand
small indignities that I had to face to make ends meet, one after
another with no relief in sight. I overdrafted my bank account
when Marie deposited a child support check on Thursday night
instead of Friday morning when my paycheck registered. Panicked, I called my bank and asked to have the insufficient-funds
fee waived. I made it a point to keep the desperation out of my
voice while trying to be as polite as humanly possible. While I was
right that asking nicely would get me out of the fee (this time), I

had barely dodged losing my grocery budget for the week. I was at the mercy of people taking pity upon me and bending the rules.

This is the situation that society tells you only happens to the irresponsible, to the poorly prepared and foolish. Yet here I was, a professional with a master's degree and an empty pantry. I could speak three languages, but I couldn't come up with the money to feed myself. Eating a free hot dog at a Wednesday-night social in a church I didn't attend, I looked across the room at the homeless men who had filed in with the crowd and wondered how many events separated their circumstances from mine. Five? A dozen? It wasn't a large number.

I wish I could say that I found a Zen balance in frugal living, but deprivation and simplicity are two very different things. It is a privilege to be able to live simply. Poverty makes every financial decision complicated. Buying food in bulk is only possible if you can afford to buy it in the first place. Making the same simple meals each week is great if you aren't forced to scour every grocery ad to see what will fit in your meager budget. When you are poor, if it's not *on* sale, it's not *for* sale.

I had to juggle my work schedule, visits with Alex, finances, and simple chores like cleaning. I sometimes had to choose between paying to wash my clothes at my apartment's laundry room and buying food.

I had found every possible way to conceal my situation from the people around me. Gone were the days when I could duck out for lunch at work, replaced by days when I brought sandwiches from home. I told coworkers I was being thrifty. When work sent me on a three-day trip with my team, my boss marveled when I turned down going out to dinner with the team in favor of a loaf of bread and a jar of peanut butter that I had packed in my suitcase. I insisted that I was watching my calories, but the reality was much grimmer. I couldn't afford a meal at a restaurant. I couldn't afford lunch out. Not once a month. Not on a special occasion. Not ever.

I thought that I did a good job hiding it, but in little ways, people showed me that they could see my desperation. A coworker won a Walmart gift card in a church raffle and slipped it to me. My boss paid for a lunch on a different trip out of town for training. A senior supervisor insisted that his wife wanted new dishes and gave me a set of plates and bowls. At every turn, people who were close to me took pity on me, and while their charity couldn't fix my situation, at least now I had more than two plates from the local dollar store.

Days at home were always confusing. With very few possessions in my apartment, there wasn't much to do, and with no money, I had nowhere to go. I would usually try to fill these days with video games and cleaning, catching up on the chores that I couldn't do on other days. Looking on my app, I saw that I was a few rides away from achieving the $200 bonus for new drivers. With some extra money burning a hole in my pocket, I decided it was time to give myself a reward for my hard work—I bought a cheap, ugly table from the local Goodwill.

I dragged it into the middle of the empty room that was supposed to be a dining area and tucked the two chairs I owned under it. It matched nothing about my apartment. I loved it anyway. A place for me to sit while I ate, rather than standing in the kitchen. It felt more like a luxury than a basic furnishing. I poured myself a drink and sat down—*sat*, what luxury—imagining myself sharing dinner with a friend. We'd laugh and talk and reminisce about better times.

I made a bowl of instant noodles and sat back down at the table. The path forward was reasonably clear. Work, drive, and parent. Conserve my resources and use the money from driving to get back the basics of a functional life. There wasn't much there that resembled the life I'd imagined, but I would have to learn to embrace a different kind of existence if I was going to get through this.

•  •  •

After work one Monday, I went home, changed clothes, and signed on to Uber. The map lit up in unfamiliar hexagons of color with percentages: a surge. The colors indicated areas with heightened demand but a shortage of drivers. The bigger the imbalance, the redder the map became. To balance things out, the app began charging more, and drivers were given a percentage bonus if they took a ride from that area. Depending on which hexagon I occupied on the map when the ping came through, I could see my earnings increased by as little as 10 percent or more than triple the normal rate.[1] I pulled out of my apartment complex and got to work. Fighting against the remnants of rush hour traffic, I landed only a few rides with the bonus before it disappeared.

The students I'd seen were quiet and unassuming, polite but mostly concerned with looking at their phones rather than talking. The pace was steady, but the rides were usually short, meaning that I was only earning the minimum fare, a little over $3, for ten to fifteen minutes of driving. This lasted until I dropped a young man off at the FSU library. The sky darkened, and one of Tallahassee's regular afternoon downpours began.

With the tropical rain pounding down on the windshield, my map immediately turned a bright red. Students, it turned out, could not stand to get wet. I watched my income for each ride double, then nearly triple. I picked up a trio of rides before the rain stopped and my map returned to the normal color. With my account showing more than enough money for one afternoon, I decided to call it a day.

As I headed home, I wondered if I was doing this right. The students were frequent riders, but I made more money on longer rides. I had no way of knowing the best way of moving forward, and the app was no help at all. The official advice said to take any ride you were offered, but unless there was a surge, there was no information about which areas were experiencing demand or how to find longer rides rather than short trips.

The silence was confusing because it was total. Uber surely had all the data about rides and demand, but there was no indication that they were willing to share any of it. Instead, I was left to guess about the best places to be and how to maximize my earnings. The "GO" button blinked at me from my dashboard, a source of mystery and frustration. Go where? All I wanted was to make enough money to survive, to help myself and my son. The app, for all its opportunities, presented only stubborn indifference.

When I logged back on for Wednesday's driving, I found a blank map. No surge. For the next few hours, I tooled around town, burning gas but barely making money. Discouraged, I went home and fixed myself a bowl of ramen noodles. Idle curiosity burned in me as I slurped down my dinner, and I wondered if I had done something wrong. I reopened the app to see if I had missed something.

The map loaded, then froze for a moment. A bright red overlay covered the entire area around FSU, centered around a series of bars that locals called "The Strip." Seizing the opportunity,

I tossed my bowl in the sink and headed back out to my car. I drove onto campus before logging back on, chasing the surge. As I picked up my first passengers for double money at 9 p.m., I asked the girls piling into my backseat what had everyone suddenly going out.

"It's White Trash!" they told me, as if I knew what that meant. Confused, I drove them to The Strip and discovered that the area was packed with students. An electronic sign on the corner advertised a weekly event I'd never noticed: White Trash Wednesdays. I shuttled a few more carloads of students to the area before calling it a night. What had started as a disappointing day had become far more profitable once the sun went down.

The people I saw that night were excited to go out, but there didn't seem to be anything unusual about them other than the occasional pair of overalls and a lot of girls in tied-up flannel shirts. The students were a lot more talkative than they had been during the afternoon, but they were also surrounded by their friends rather than going back and forth to class. That small sample of the party life of FSU did not prepare me for what was coming. My first real Friday shift was equal parts jaw-dropping and eye-opening. After a quick jaunt home after work to eat, shower, and change into casual clothes, I made a peanut butter and jelly sandwich for the road, picked up a soda while I gassed up the car, and logged on to complete chaos.

FSU students didn't just go out on Fridays, they went crazy. Students descended on local watering holes in the afternoon for cheap drinks and nominal ID checks and kept going until happy hour specials ended after 9 p.m. They'd call for rides to go back to their apartments or dorms just long enough to shower, eat something, and change clothes before heading back to dance at nightclubs until they closed at 2 a.m. Once the clubs had shut, they'd call yet more rides to get home or go to afterparties.

If anything else was happening in Tallahassee that Friday, I missed it entirely. From the moment I logged on, I was barraged with ride requests, with a ping for the next ride often coming in just moments after I picked up my rider. The map burned bright red for most of the night, and I could barely find time to take breaks amid the chaos of constant pickups, drop-offs, and pings. Every watering hole around the campus sported lines of students that stretched outside and down the block, and groups of kids could be seen weaving drunkenly down the sidewalks on every corner.

Amid the constant demand were the riders themselves. With no idea what to expect going in, I hadn't set the boundaries that I needed for how I would expect people to behave in my car, and while most students were well-behaved (if very drunk), a few pushed the limits. With no regard for me, riders rolled windows down to spit into the street, turned my radio up to deafening levels, and fiddled with the heat as if it were their car, not mine.

While the rides were mostly the same (from an apartment to a bar, or vice versa), the college students showed me a lifestyle that I had always assumed was limited to movie depictions of fraternity parties. Groups of young men stumbled into my backseat, slurring their words as they asked me if I had an aux cord so they could play their own music. Young women dressed in very little despite the chill weather openly discussed their plans for who to sleep with that night if their first choice was too drunk.

My first argument with a rider foreshadowed what would become a constant battle with the students over the limits of my vehicle. It was nearly 11 p.m. when I pulled into an apartment parking lot and saw Paul break off from a group standing outside to walk toward my car, his friends in tow.[2] A beer in his hand, he had curly brown hair tucked under a backward baseball cap with a cigarette tucked behind one ear and a joint behind the other. He hopped into the passenger seat and let out a belch before he turned to look at me.

"Yo, is it cool if we squeeze a couple?" Paul asked.

It took me several moments to answer, during which his friends began to pile into the backseat. He felt like a caricature straight out of a comedy sketch, yet there he was, right in front of me. I told Paul that we couldn't fit six people in my car, and some of his tightly packed friends would need to get out. Amid the immediate outburst of complaints from the backseat, he lifted up his hat to smooth down his hair.

"Dawg, everybody lets people squeeze," Paul insisted, clearly trying to be convincing despite slurring his words. "You got a big car. What's the problem?"

I told him that everyone had to be able to wear a seatbelt, and it wouldn't be safe for people to "squeeze" by packing into the backseat. If we got into an accident, his friends would get hurt. This last point drew a round of complaints from the liquored-up men in the backseat. They insisted that we weren't going far, and besides, nothing was going to happen.

I felt that I was striking a delicate balance. The young men were full of liquid courage and youthful testosterone. I didn't want to create a confrontation between myself and six people, but I couldn't give them what they wanted. I'd seen other cars that night that would stop and let loose a half dozen students like some sort of university-themed clown car, but it wasn't a risk I wanted to take. If Paul got out and canceled the ride, I would get $3.85 of the $5 cancellation fee, but that would be far less compared to the money I'd make if I just drove them all where they wanted. I decided to stand firm and told him that we could only take three in the backseat.

"What about the trunk?" one of the young men asked. I immediately snapped at him that no one was riding in the trunk. Defeated, Paul relented, and after a brief discussion, several of the young men climbed out. I let Paul finish his beer before we left, his extra friends standing on the curb ordering a second car as he tossed the can into some nearby bushes. Although he was memorable, the argument that I'd had with him was one that I would have every weekend for the next few years.

Except for a few small windows of time when students were preparing for their next pitstop, the surge indicated double, triple, and even higher multipliers on rides. Staying out until the bars closed, I made more than I'd taken in during the previous two days of driving combined, sometimes earning as much as $30 per hour for short hops around the campus. Two weeks ago, I'd been standing behind a register worrying if I would be able to make the rent. Now, I was earning more per hour than I was at my day job with half the effort. Buzzing with caffeine but exhausted from my long day, I went home, poured myself a drink, and reflected on the night.

There had been fun moments. Passengers sometimes sang along to songs on the radio, and most of them were drunk but courteous. I was doing them a favor by giving them a ride, and that encouraged them to be nice to me. Since I circled campus constantly, I could tell students if the line at their destination was long, and they seemed to really appreciate that. The gratitude made me feel useful, which was a nice change of pace from my life outside of the car.

I saw bad things too. The fraternity brothers seemed especially rude, but most students were more interested in getting from place to place than causing trouble. Students often waited to even start walking down from their buildings until I'd been waiting outside for several minutes, which meant I spent a lot of time sitting in parking lots waiting for people who might not show up. I'd had to tell several people to either chug their beers or leave them behind before we could get going. I wasn't going to risk my car smelling like stale spilled beer just because a bunch of kids couldn't put the party on hold to travel a few miles.

Overall, the money was better than expected around campus. Yeah, some people were rude, but people I'd encountered in retail had been rude just as often. I'd survived in that environment by focusing on the work and the fact that I had to survive. If driving was going to earn this kind of money, my days of worrying about rent were over. It didn't matter if I liked them or not, the money was with the students. I poured myself a second drink.

*Yeah. This works for now.*

# 3

THE NEXT FEW MONTHS WERE A BLUR OF WORKING, DRIVING, AND PARENTING.
With my money situation improved, I was able to pay attention to
the things I had neglected since the divorce. I saw an eye doctor
and got new glasses. I bought Alex a shiny green bike for Christmas and jogged alongside him as he rode to the end of the street
and back, wobbling on the training wheels. More money also
meant a bigger grocery budget. I was still living paycheck to paycheck, but at least now I could afford pizza every now and then.

My initial joy at the hourly wages I was earning was quickly
offset by a return to the baseline of driving. There was a narrow
window on Friday nights when I could earn good money for a
short period of time, but this was the exception. On most days
and nights, that sort of money wasn't possible, and the only way
to make up the difference was to spend even more time on the
app. I convinced myself that I was "on the grind," working hard
now so that I could relax in the future.

That sort of toxic "hustle culture" is ubiquitous in America,
but it neglects the very real desire for human connection for
which so many people yearn. My passengers were often single
riders on their way to social events. They would arrive by themselves and leave by themselves, and in between, they would tell

themselves they were not lonely. Perhaps they could have carpooled with friends or designated a driver for their night out, but in our modern, hyperindividual world, their social lives were too fragmented to navigate that relationship.

After some rides, passengers would ask if there was a way they could request me again. No, I would tell them, you press the button, and you get what the app decides. The only way to arrange it would have been to give them my phone number and arrange a cash ride "off the books," something I wasn't willing to do. As much as I enjoyed the human contact that driving provided, my nights, just like theirs, always ended the same way that they began: alone.

Driving became my life. I forced myself to take the occasional Monday night off (business was bad then anyway), but every other hour I was awake was filled with work: breakfast, day job, a quick change of clothes, then straight out and onto the app. While I mourned the death of the weekend, I told myself that the long hours were worth it. I was paying off debts I had racked up during the divorce, and if things kept up, I'd be able to start taking more days off.

My inability to make ends meet without a second job wasn't unique; it was part of a growing trend. For the past twenty years, the number of Americans working multiple jobs has risen steadily.[1] A 2014 Gallup survey found that 13 percent of Americans reported working two or more jobs. For those working just one job, the hours had grown longer without a rise in compensation. The forty-hour workweek, once a staple of American society, had been obliterated. Fully half of American workers told the survey that they worked more than forty hours, with 39 percent reporting workweeks of more than fifty hours.[2] As the US Census Bureau delicately put it, "Having more than one job shows a talent in time management." In reality, overworked Americans didn't have much choice, and over time, many of our social networks and interactions revolved more around work life.

This was the loneliest period of my life. The companionship of friends and a partner that I had known every day for so many years was gone, replaced with solitary nights and the occasional presence of a toddler. My safety net had been shredded, and my support network was badly eroded. The pressure began to wear on me, and I slowly crumpled under the withering loneliness.

With more money coming in from driving, I found myself stopping at the local liquor store on occasion to pick up a large bottle of cheap bourbon and a carton of ginger ale. What started as an occasional drink when I got home began to evolve into a regular habit. Even before kicking my shoes off, I'd crack open a soda and pour myself a triple. Once the glass was empty enough to pour the rest of the ginger ale in, I'd add another shot or two to make sure I could make my feelings stop. On most nights, my alcohol intake could most easily be measured in how many cans I went through. Most nights there were two, but I could sometimes handle a third before I fell asleep.

On one particularly lonely night, I called every single contact in my phone's address book. An old college classmate was the only one to pick up. Quickly realizing how intoxicated I was, he made polite conversation as I slurred before excusing himself. I ended up falling asleep at my thrift store table, the empty glass sitting beside me as I snored, too drunk to make even the short walk to my bed. I often stumbled into the walls as I tried to walk between the couch and the kitchen for a refill. With the room delightfully tilting, I would sing what little I could remember from the pop songs that filled the radio when I was driving. My neighbors surely hated me.

In the mornings, I'd awaken to the sound of my alarm clock, clean up the empty soda cans, and try to eat something to offset the headache that was becoming my daily companion on the ride to work. The first few hours of each day were spent doing the simplest, quietest work that I could find. My aching head had no ability to do anything else.

Somewhere inside of me was the knowledge that what I was doing was unhealthy, but it was offset by my desire for emotional oblivion. To feel nothing was preferable to the storm that raged inside me. I had never struggled with alcohol in the past, but as I did the best I could to process what had gone wrong, some dark part of me craved obliteration. The person I needed to be for others, for my job, and for my son crowded out time that I could have spent working through my personal demons. With no time for myself, I found it was easier to drown the feelings in a tide of brown liquor, consequences be damned.

There was, however, one regular presence that ironically comforted me. Night after night, I turned on the app and waited for the brief moments of human contact that would happen between the times people climbed in and out of the car. I came to love the moments of candor that people shared with me, the polite kindness that they would show me. It meant a lot simply to have someone be nice to me. I had no illusions about the origin of these niceties. I was giving them a ride, giving them something they wanted or needed, and their appreciation was based largely on my ability to fulfill their needs. Although some people were rude or quiet, it was easier to forget them and focus on those who provided me with the social interaction I desperately needed.

As the tech-driven economy increasingly moved people's lives into curated online spaces, it was comforting to me to interact in a physical space, in a place where riders could not present themselves in filtered perfection. Social media is filled with false portrayals of lives where nothing is ever wrong, but in the backseat of a car, the messy reality bled out everywhere. Girls with Instagram feeds full of fashion and brunch pics would sob to me about their cheating boyfriends and backstabbing besties. Young men expressed doubts about the tiresome masculinity they were forced to perform for their friends. We were a captive audience for each other's doubts, and while not everyone wanted to talk, so many of them wanted nothing more than to voice their fears out loud, to know that another human being would hear them. They could admit these things in the quiet darkness of the night, lit up only by passing streetlights, and when we arrived, they would take a selfie in the backseat and get back to trying to look perfect for an audience of strangers.

Driving people to and from the events of their lives allowed me to piggyback on their successes and failures. I couldn't afford to go to a football game, but I could drop someone off and pretend that someday it would be my turn. Someday, I would go out on a Friday night to meet my friends. Surely those days couldn't be too far away.

．  ．  ．

I left work on a Wednesday afternoon in April and logged on to the app to find myself assigned to pick up Diane. Requesting a short ride, Diane only needed to run to a nearby liquor store and back to her house. Dressed in shorts and a tank top, she had a sallow, sunken look in her eyes that spoke of a long, terrible day.

From the moment she got in, I could tell she had something on her mind, but my few attempts to get her to talk were unsuccessful. The tension built as we rolled through her neighborhood, finally coming to a boiling point as we halted at a red light.

"My son almost died today," she blurted out.

Unsure what to say, I told her I was sorry. As we cruised through the streets toward her destination, the story poured out. Her son had moved home from New York to try to beat a heroin habit he'd developed after getting hooked on pain pills when he broke his leg in a car accident. He'd stayed clean for months before relapsing. Diane had found him on the couch that morning, a needle sitting in his lap. She'd called me because she'd just gotten home from the hospital. He'd lived, and she needed a drink. I tried to comfort her between her choking sobs, but I had no idea what to say. The thought of losing a child was so immense that any words I might have had felt small in comparison.

As we arrived at the liquor store, she thanked me for listening and went inside, emerging a few minutes later with a brown bag filled with whatever relief she'd purchased. As she climbed back into the car, I told her that I hoped tomorrow would be better. She cried quietly on the ride home, clearly overwhelmed with processing the events of her day. As we pulled into the driveway, she leaned over the center console suddenly and hugged me. I told her that things would be okay, and she held onto me, shaking as she sobbed.

When she finally let go of me, she apologized through red eyes, collected her bag, and left to drink herself into oblivion. I swiped the app to end the ride and pulled down the street to think about what had just happened. The app chimed with another ride for me. I stared at it as the timer counted down before tapping the "X" to ignore the ride. I logged off and drove home, already craving a drink of my own.

Sometimes, one ride was enough.

Deep down, I knew what I probably needed was a good therapist, but mental health resources in Tallahassee, much like the rest of America, were limited. There's a shortage of psychologists and psychiatrists in America, with an analysis by the American Association of Medical Colleges concluding that more than 150 million Americans live in an area that the federal government deems to have a "mental health professional shortage."[3] The insurance I had through my day job covered a limited pool of providers, many of whom were not accepting new patients. Some required me to pay upfront and submit receipts for reimbursement through my health insurance provider, an extra step I had neither the time nor the free cash flow to pursue. With money in short supply, the best I could do was connect for a brief moment with the strangers in my backseat. They would talk to me about their lives, and I could offer them my advice. I could draw on my own experiences to try to solve their problems, and occasionally I could test out talking about my own situation.

The immense shame I felt about the divorce, failing in my marriage, and being reduced to such meager circumstances wasn't something I could stand to talk about often, but every time someone new got into the car, I had another opportunity to practice being a different person. As passenger after passenger asked me why I had become a driver, I was forced to confront and desensitize myself to the pain of admitting that I was divorced. Even saying the words "I'm divorced" out loud was enough to make my emotions well up inside me at first, but after months of practice, I had become accustomed to just saying the words and watching for a reaction.

Most people gave some measure of sympathy, and a few told stories of their own. Middle-aged men usually took it as an opportunity to talk about their own divorces, while women wished me happiness for the future. No one gave me the harsh judgment that I felt I deserved, and eventually, I was able to convince myself that perhaps I shouldn't think of myself as a *total* failure. It wasn't therapy, but it was something.

In between these moments when I forced myself into confronting reality were all the times I simply pretended to be someone else. With my baby-faced appearance, I was often assumed to be in my mid-twenties. People asked if I was a student at the university, and at times I went along with it. I was a graduate student in meteorology, you see, trying to find a better way to detect tornadoes. I was an accountant for a local business, drumming up some extra cash. I was a full-time driver. An aspiring stand-up comedian. Anything was better than the truth.

I explored all the people I might have been if I had lived a different life. I tried on the identities of people whose lives hadn't gone awry, people who were successful or striving or hoping. I told strangers that I was saving up for a vacation, that I was going to backpack across Europe or visit a Japanese hot spring. Every person in the backseat became an opportunity to imagine a better life.

This chameleon act was useful for the nights when I couldn't bear to think about my situation, but sometimes I wanted to close my eyes and indulge in the fantasy that nothing was wrong. Those were the nights when I took my old wedding ring out of the box in my closet and slipped it on for the night. When passengers asked what brought me to Tallahassee, I could answer their follow-up questions about whether I was still with my girlfriend by tapping my hand on the back of the headrest to show off the golden band around my finger. The college girls found this particularly thrilling, and I basked in their adoration at my commitment. When they asked why I was driving, I told them that I was earning extra money for the down payment on our dream home.

I would take the ring on and off throughout the night, gliding between telling the truth and the lie that I wished could have been. On weeks when I was strong, I would test my limits by telling people more of the truth. Rather than stuffing my emotions down inside of me, I would let them peek out, little by little. When I was inevitably overwhelmed, I could slip the ring on my finger and disappear into the identity of a man who wasn't ashamed.

I didn't like lying, but in the face of my internal turmoil, it was better to take two steps forward and one step back than to continue suppressing my emotions. With no place to process what I had gone through, I dealt with my emotions behind the wheel. It was a place where I was in charge, where I was both literally and metaphorically in the driver's seat. I didn't have the strength to tell the truth all the time, but telling it some of the time was better than how I had started.

The reactions of the college students were by far the most comforting. While older men would sometimes rant hatefully about their exes and couples would awkwardly change the subject, the students simply accepted me. At times, their own lives were as complicated as mine. This was the case near the end of the academic year when I picked up Sandra and her friends.

The three girls were dressed in sparkling gowns, clutching small purses and wobbling in heels that were too high for their level of intoxication. As I watched them stumble toward the car, I slipped my ring off and stashed it in the center console. They looked friendly, and I assumed I wouldn't need my golden talisman's protection from a group of sorority girls on their way to some sort of formal event.

Sandra climbed into the middle of the backseat, taking a moment to scoot the shimmery fabric down as she settled in between her friends. Mere moments after they piled in, the predictable questions started. Was I from Tallahassee? How long had I been driving? Was I still with the girl who had brought me to the city? I took a moment to breathe before telling them that we had gotten divorced the previous year.

"Oh, my parents are divorced," one of the friends chimed in. The other nodded sagely beside me and told me that hers were too, and it had turned out okay. As her friends told me that it was too bad and they were sorry for me, Sandra chose a different route.

"Did you guys have any kids?" she asked. Yes, I said, tapping the home button on my phone to show off the picture of Alex that served as my background. Sandra's friends cooed that he was cute.

"Just make sure that he knows you still love him," she said. Sandra went on to say that her parents were divorced, and she had been dealing with them fighting about who would come to her graduation. Two grown adults despised each other so much that they couldn't bear the sight of one another for even a few hours to celebrate the accomplishment of their own child. She said it was yet another episode in a long line of one-sided holidays where she'd had to play peacemaker. As she spoke, her friends passed her tissues to save her from smearing her eye makeup with her tears.

"Most of the time it's not so bad. It was only a big deal at, like, Christmas. That's when I really wished we could have been together."

I told her that I wasn't going to have that sort of relationship with Marie. Even if we weren't together anymore, I didn't want us to be enemies. I'd never wanted that, not for us or for Alex. I hated the middle-aged men who spoke scornfully of their ex-wives. No matter what had passed between us, Marie was my son's mother, and that alone made her worthy of respect. Sandra told me that she wished her parents could have had my attitude. Perhaps that was the reason she had joined the sorority in the first place, to try to find the sense of family that she had lacked as a teenager.

I dropped the young women off at the colossal brick stadium of FSU for whatever formal event was being hosted there. My next ride was already waiting for me just a few blocks away. As I rolled up, I looked down at the center console and thought about the ring inside. I wondered about Alex, asleep at the house. Did he miss me when I was out working? Did he wake up wondering where I was? Would he tell his friends that his parents were happier apart, or would he pine for us to be together again?

I looked down at a black stuffed bear that sat in my cupholder. A toy from a McDonald's happy meal, it had come from a promotion for endangered animals. I carried it with me in the car as a symbol of Alex. Ever since he'd been born, he'd been my little bear. The stuffed animal was my way of taking him with me wherever I went. I picked up the little bear as I waited for my passengers and thought about Sandra's words.

*It's only a big deal at, like, Christmas.*

I sure hoped so.

# CHAPTER 4

"ARE YOU ALRIGHT?"

I felt my head jerk up from my chest at the sound of someone talking to me. It was the middle of the afternoon at the office, and I was supposed to be listening in on a conference call with the FBI.

"Are you okay?" came the whispered voice again. It was an older analyst in our unit named Robert, a former police officer who had retired into an analytical role. Since his desk was next to mine, Robert saw more of me than anyone else in the squad bay. He had years of experience sifting through evidence for minute clues, but he didn't need that to see what was going on: I was exhausted.

Sitting in a chair with a notepad in my lap, I'd tried desperately to stay awake as the call droned on. I'd pinched myself, changed my position endlessly, and tried taking scrupulous notes about the discussion, but nothing could beat back the tiredness that was consuming me. In the after-lunch warmth of the conference room, my eyelids had eventually begun to sag.

I nodded in a panic, wondering how long I had dozed.

"You were snoring," Robert whispered. I glanced across the room to my boss, an older woman who had been more patient

41

with me during my divorce than I could possibly have deserved. She glared back at me, her eyes conveying what her voice couldn't in the situation. I shifted uncomfortably in the hard plastic chair as my anxiety jolted me awake. When the call wrapped up a few minutes later, my boss asked me to stay behind as the rest of the attendees filed out of the room.

Even before she started talking, I was consumed with worry. I tried to imagine how I would ever survive if I lost my job. I could turn to driving full-time while I looked for another job, but everything that I'd seen so far showed me that I wouldn't even be able to tread water if I did that. What followed after my boss closed the door was equal parts getting chewed out for embarrassing her and questions about my well-being.

Her concerns were well founded. The more I drove, the less I slept. The less I slept, the more caffeine I needed just to function, and the more caffeine I drank, the more I tried to counteract the stimulation with alcohol. Between coffee in the mornings and sodas in the afternoon, the sheer amount of caffeine I was pouring into my system just to stay awake would probably have seemed impossible to me a few months ago. I tried not to think about the stress it was putting on my heart and pushed aside the knowledge that my mother's family had a history of cardiac problems.

As my boss urged me to take better care of myself, she told me that she had noticed the quality of my work declining. She could only see the output, but her instincts were correct. I was working through each day on autopilot. In the mornings, I was too hungover to concentrate. By the afternoon, I was too exhausted to be productive. I told her that I would try to get more rest.

"Good," she told me as she opened the door to go back to her desk. "I can't cover for you forever."

. . .

My identity had become so intertwined with my work that I could no longer identify myself. I had worked so hard for so long just to survive that I didn't know how to switch off survival mode and be myself. What did "being myself" even mean? Was the chatty, joke-telling Uber driver the real me? The sober, analytical man at the office? The broken person who stared in the mirror before stumbling off to a mattress on the floor?

How did my son see me? When I asked him what Daddy did for work, his answers alternated between saying I was the Taxi Man (a term he coined when I first described my driving to him) and thinking I was a police officer. I didn't know how to correct him, because I no longer knew the answer myself. Instead, I focused my time with him on making memories that would last until I could rediscover what it meant to be a whole person. As long as he knew that I loved him, that would be enough.

The very idea of being something felt alien, for all I really wanted was to be taken away from the looming feeling that I was about to tumble off a cliff and lose everything. I had no more dreams, no more ambitions. In their place was a numb, hollowed-out body with one urgent command: survive.

My day-to-day life was precarious, but it was no different from what millions of other Americans experienced every day. The more I drove, the more solidarity I felt with my working-class passengers. In my eyes, I no longer had much in common with the middle-class riders who used rideshare as a way to go to and from social events and date nights. For every wealthy couple I picked up from a fancy restaurant, there were twice as many workers who lay in the backseat in exhaustion. I saw my reflection in their worn-down, sallow faces. I had never worked in food service, but my time in retail taught me that people can be petty and cruel for no reason when they know their victim can't fight back. I tried my hardest to be patient with and kind to the people in Walmart vests and fast-food uniforms, to the single mothers and public housing residents who had no cars but had to work lest their benefits be revoked. I installed my car seat for their children and waited for them while they ran into the local dollar store to shop for groceries. When rides like these ended, I sometimes tapped around on the app and refunded them. It felt cruel to take the last dollars of those who had so little. I knew what could be bought with ten or fifteen dollars, and it was far more important than the six bucks that would have been my share.

My own experiences in deprivation had been defined by endless small indignities that bled away my ego in a thousand cuts. My horizon shrank, and I found that I could not plan for the future because of the fierce urgency of *now*.

I understood why people would do everything in their power to hide the sacrifices they were making from their children. Alex and I spent endless afternoons at free places. We would go to the local mall and ride the escalators up and down for an hour before splitting a pretzel. We came up with a color-coded system for referring to the best playgrounds based on the color of the equipment. The red and blue park had better slides, but the green and blue park had more things to climb on. Our days were filled with pretend adventures and running errands, anything to avoid requests to go places that might cost money. The limit of my ability to indulge him was usually a kid's meal from McDonald's, and my apartment soon brimmed with the endless cheap, plastic toys that came with them.

I never breathed a word of my situation to Alex. He was far too young to understand, and when I was too exhausted to play, I would ask him to play quietly while I took a nap on the couch. I hated using a kid's movie to babysit him, but I often needed to rest in order to muster the strength to go driving once he was tucked into bed. With every bedtime story, I reminded myself of why I was sacrificing.

My working hours had synced up with the constant tempo of special events at FSU, but as I approached the end of April, I began to notice a dip in my earnings. Most Friday nights had been filled with students calling rides despite the surging rates, and their willingness to call a ride for any reason had filled my wallet. As the month wore on, I noticed that the surges came less and less frequently, and slowly my nightly take decreased.

At first, I attributed the drop in business to final exams, but as graduation parties finished up and the city began to empty, I had to face facts: the students were leaving. In a city of barely two hundred thousand residents, more than thirty thousand of the most reliable customers I could have wished for were going home for the summer. Unsure of what things would look like once they were gone, I was given a glimpse when Cinco de Mayo fell on a Friday.

Tooling around town with margarita-filled locals in my back-seat, I couldn't help but notice that the price surges I had come to rely on were gone. Instead of a constant barrage of ride re-quests, I found myself sitting in parking lots for fifteen to twenty minutes between rides. The locals tended to need to go further than the students, and although that made up some of the dif-ference in rates, I still saw a significant drop in my earnings. A night when I usually made about $140 was finished with a lackluster $100.

I tried to bargain with myself, rationalizing that $40 here or there wouldn't break me. I could make up the difference during the week by doing a few extra hours of driving on the days when I wasn't with Alex. If I cut back a little bit on my groceries, it would be okay. I was lucky that my utility bill every month was rock bottom, a consequence of turning off the air conditioning any time I wasn't at home (which was most of the time).

What I found the next week was even worse. During the weekdays, I found myself sitting in parking lots more and more frequently, sometimes waiting as long as an hour for a ride to appear. Other than a quick burst of activity during rush hour after work, requests ground to a halt. When the app dinged, I would race for my customers and the few dollars that driving them would give me. By the time Friday arrived, I was preparing myself for the worst.

I told myself that Friday night would make up for the slow week I had just endured, that I would be able to make up the difference, but after leaving work at 5 p.m. and immediately getting on the road, I had barely managed to scrape up $90 by 1 a.m. It had been obvious that things would be different when the students left town, but I hadn't understood that the change would be so drastic. As I gave up and headed home, I had to accept that things would be different during the summer.

Pouring myself a drink to try to counteract all the caffeine I had ingested while driving, I ran through the numbers. There were a few places where I could cut back, but no amount of belt tightening was going to fill the gap of several hundred dollars that this slowdown was going to create. With rising panic, I realized that the hours I was working would have to change.

Over the past few months, I had settled into a rhythm of driving until I'd made $20 a few nights during the week, then seeing what I could earn on the weekends when I wasn't with Alex. With Friday bringing in $120–$150, I'd only have to put in a few more hours on a Saturday night or Sunday afternoon to reach my goal of $250. Most weeks, I was making around $300 before I got tired and headed home.

This all added up to fifteen to twenty hours per week behind the wheel, with the bulk of that time spent in one long run on Friday nights. It was a long and brutal shift for me to work one job during the day and another until the bars closed, but that was my window for making the best money. Sometimes I could get lucky and hit my goal in as little as twelve hours, but now I was going to have to live in the driver's seat just to make things work.

It dawned on me that more driving would be like sailing with the wind against me. The more hours I sat behind the wheel, the more gas I burned. The more gas I burned, the more I needed to budget for fuel, and that was even more money that I had to earn. I was facing a Sisyphean task, desperately trying to take one step forward without sliding two steps back.

I tried different strategies for finding riders, including checking the flight schedules to try to catch people arriving at the airport. Landing an airport ride could mean big money if the passenger needed to go a long way, but it was also a big gamble. If my passenger was headed to a downtown hotel, the ride would only earn me $8. Sitting in the airport parking lot with other Uber drivers also meant risking that the rides would dry up before it was my turn for the app to ding. I was sacrificing huge amounts of time for an uncertain payout.

My next option was big-box retailers. I'd picked up passengers from Walmart in the past, and nothing about the summertime made people need groceries any less. Much to my frustration, the rides that I could land were always short and required waiting while people moved a dozen bags in and out of my trunk. I would spend half an hour on one ride to make $4. No one goes across town to buy their groceries.

Between the uncertain gambles of the airport and the weak but certain flow of grocery trips was my eventual solution. My day job had taught me to be thoughtful and analytical, and I used the data I was collecting every time someone got in my car to figure out where I needed to be. I began to note the times of day when certain areas of town were busy, paying careful attention to exactly who was in the backseat. I memorized the closing hours for different shopping centers and the shift changes of the local hospitals.

A nurse at a local psychiatric office always went to yoga at 5:30, just a few minutes after I left the office myself. A woman at a call center got off work at 6. If I missed her, a local government office that arranged services for blind people had a very polite lady who needed a ride across town every day around 6:15. A local mechanic would call rides to take customers home after they dropped their cars off at the end of the day. After that, the nurses at the hospital would rotate on their shifts. By the time I got someone home from the hospital, it was time for people to start leaving restaurants. An hour later, the stores started to close. The entire pattern was a gamble, but I was able to nail it with enough frequency to stay afloat. Gone were the heady days of driving a college student half a mile for double pay, replaced with days when I hoped that the Wednesday-night karaoke crowd would need a ride.

I thought back on the ads I'd seen that promised that I could work when I wanted and be my own boss. Uber's ads had promised me a world of on-demand employment, a world where I could press a button and start earning money. The slick ads on Uber's website and across the internet had sworn that I could make hundreds of dollars each week, that drivers in major cities were making fantastic salaries on their own schedule. I'd become accustomed to the idea that I would have to work a little harder than the ads said to make the money I needed, but I was unprepared for my entire solution to stop working. I felt I had not just been misled by glossy advertising; I had been lied to about the whole experience. Scrambling for the few meager dollars I could scrape up, I didn't feel like I was in charge of anything.

I went back to the local Facebook group I had initially canvassed for advice to ask if this was normal. The answers were disheartening. A few people responded that I should quit and leave them more business. They blamed an influx of rookie drivers for the inability to make decent money. Others made it clear that this was the norm for the summer months. One poster joked that I should switch to delivering pizzas.

As I filled my nights with working (and then drinking), I found myself wondering why I had to work so hard just to have so little. It shouldn't have been this hard to make a living, to have a little safety for myself and my son. As week after week went by, my work hours had mushroomed while my bank account had stagnated. If hard work was supposed to be the key to success, I was baffled by my inability to meet my own basic needs. I had done everything that society told me should guarantee a decent life: I'd gone to college (twice!), found a steady job, and worked hard. Somehow, it wasn't enough. I had been raised to believe that education was the key to success, to a good job and a stable income, but it just wasn't true. One report published in 2015 found that 48 percent of drivers had at least a college degree, above the national average.[1] For them, just like me, education had done little to guarantee security.

My anger was tempered somewhat by the fact that I had been able to keep my promise to Alex. Week after week, I was able to give Marie the money I had promised so that Alex could have the things I wanted for him: a house to call home, the security of a stable environment, and hopefully, a future that would be better than my present circumstances. I did not relish my return to a poverty so deep that I had to choose between groceries and washing my clothes, but I would do it for Alex. I consoled myself with stiff drinks and the belief that all of this was temporary.

I had put up with so many things by this point that I thought driving couldn't possibly hold any surprises for me. When passengers asked me about my wildest experiences, I had plenty of stories to share. I'd even secured a $150 cleaning fee from Uber during the school year when a drunken sorority girl had urinated on herself in my backseat. I'd soaked up the stain using an entire roll of paper towels, spritzed my backseat with air freshener, and gone right back to driving, thankful that the years of experience with diaper changes had eliminated any squeamishness I might have had about bodily fluids.

Still, there was one major thing that had never happened, the thing that I had always expected would come at the hands of a liquored-up college student. To date, I had managed to avoid having anyone throw up in my car. There had been close calls, but I usually managed to direct the dry heaving college students to the trash bag I kept in the seat back. One young man had held it together until he reached his destination before thanking me politely, stepping out, and projectile vomiting against the side of a building, his hands firmly on his hips as he painted the brick with the contents of his stomach. I knew it would happen someday. I had accepted it as inevitable when I signed up to do the work. What I hadn't expected was the bizarre way that it would finally occur.

Brenda was a middle-aged housewife in a black and white shift dress. I picked her up from a bar and grill that specialized in chicken wings and advertised a "Wine-Down Wednesday" event. She greeted me warmly and asked if it was alright if she sat in the passenger seat. I nodded my assent, and she waved goodbye to the friends she had met for after-work drinks. The app showed her destination as a nearby neighborhood filled with trendy McMansions, an area that I associated with the sort of upper-middle-class families that had two kids, a dog, and a hefty tuition payment for a private school. It wasn't the sort of ride that I thought would have caused trouble.

As soon as we exited the parking lot, Brenda began to fidget and swallow heavily. In a college student, I would have recognized the signs, but my guard was down. It was a Wednesday evening in the middle of the summer. The college students were gone, and I had logged on to drive after detailing my car in a gas station parking lot after work. The afternoon had passed quickly, with off-duty nurses and retail workers giving me plenty of rides. By the time the sun went down and Brenda called for a ride, I'd settled into my rhythm for the night.

We were less than a mile up the road when Brenda suddenly groaned and sent a tide of red liquid that looked alarmingly like blood onto my dashboard. It took a few moments to process what had just happened. Brenda clutched at her stomach and threw up again as she tried to apologize, the mess mostly landing on herself. I pulled down a nearby side street and stopped while Brenda rolled out of the car and scrabbled across the ground to a nearby drainage ditch to continue vomiting. A family walking their dog paused for a moment, the mother stepping forward to get a better look at the scene.

"Is she alright?" the man asked, holding the dog's leash. I shrugged and said that she might have had too much to drink. I used Brenda's absence as an opportunity to evaluate the mess inside the car. The red liquid that coated my dashboard was the remains of however many glasses of wine Brenda had consumed at the bar, mixed with whatever she had eaten with them. It dripped off the dashboard and into the floor mats in thick strings of sweet-smelling refuse. On the seat, a small pile of chunks sat in a puddle of pale pink liquid. I opened the trunk to look for cleaning supplies. To my dismay, I realized that I had used the last of my paper towels detailing the car before I logged on.

I waited for a few minutes as Brenda collected herself. The family with the dog wandered off. Brenda pulled herself out the ditch and stumbled back to the car to survey the damage she had done.

"I'm so sorry. I'll clean this up," she slurred out.

"Don't worry about it," I told her. "Let's just get you home."

"No, no. I insist."

"I'm out of paper towels," I told her, hoping that would get her in the car so that I could get rid of her. Instead, she looked around briefly before pulling her dress over her head. I sat with mouth agape as the underwear-clad housewife wiped my dashboard with her dress before sitting back down in the passenger seat. She cradled her vomit-soaked dress in her lap.

I put my eyes on the road and forced myself to focus on the driving. I passed the trash bag from my seat back to Brenda without looking and pulled up the navigation on the app. The car reeked of cheap wine and stomach acid, and I was grateful that the darkness hid Brenda's semi-nude form. I ignored the speed limits and pushed through to Brenda's house in record time. As I raced through the dark streets, Brenda alternated between stuffing her face in the trash bag to vomit and attempting to apologize.

When we finally arrived at her house, Brenda seemed to realize what her situation looked like.

"Oh fuck," she mumbled. "My kids are going to see me."

I didn't know how to tell her that I didn't care. She seemed to contemplate the situation for a moment before her addled mind hit upon a solution.

"There's a key to the back under one of the rocks in the garden. Can you light up the side so I can find it?" I pulled my car diagonally in the driveway to illuminate a landscaped patch of her yard. Brenda got out and began crawling about on her hands and knees to turn over rocks. That was when the rain started, a North Florida summer downpour, an intense soaking that would probably only last twenty minutes. It was just long enough to add insult to Brenda's injured pride.

From the interior of the car, I took pictures of my vomit-soaked seats and dashboard, mindful that Brenda might think I was taking pictures of her. The last thing I needed was more conflict with the woman who had turned my office into a toilet bowl. Brenda, soaked to the skin and cradling her stained dress, finally found the key and came to apologize to me. She offered to tip me $80 on the app. I told her that would help, but I knew she was lying. Everyone promised to tip me, but no one ever did.

I watched Brenda disappear into her backyard before I drove to the local Walmart to buy cleaning supplies. With a few taps, I submitted the pictures to Uber. I scrubbed the seats with fabric cleaner, wiped the vomit off my dashboard, and wondered how long it would take for the smell to come out. I checked back on the app and saw that Uber was sending me a direct payment for the mess. Since it involved bodily fluids, Brenda would be charged $200. I would receive $150, and Uber would keep $50 despite having experienced none of the unpleasantness involved in the altercation. It was the standard arrangement.

All told, the ride and the cleanup had taken a little over an hour. I spritzed the entire car with air freshener and set my navigation to take me home. Driving with the windows down, I took a few deep breaths and tried to figure out what to do with myself. I hadn't signed up to clean up other people's vomit, but for $150 per hour, there were a lot of things I was willing to do. Especially if it meant I got to go home early.

. . .

By the end of the summer, I was physically and mentally burned out. My nonstop work schedule and heavy-drinking habits had taken a toll, and I spent most of my days in a thick haze of exhaustion. As August neared its end, I began to see more students in my backseat. Those who lived off campus had returned to the rundown apartment complexes that ringed the university, and their need for groceries and trips to Target gave me a badly needed respite from the grueling hours of the previous months.

As I drove them around town, I kept hearing an unfamiliar phrase: "syllabus week." Such was the name given to the first week of classes, a time when the entire student body was on campus with few assignments to take up their time. The name was taken from the belief that very little happened in the first week other than professors handing out the course syllabus. Rather than get a jump on their studies, the syllabus week served as an outrageous bacchanal. Students planned their social calendars as closely as their class schedules, and even otherwise upstanding scholars would join the partying. The most antisocial bookworms partied during syllabus week.

Even with my familiarity with the outlandish antics of the FSU student body, I was unprepared for the sheer hedonism. A group of fraternity brothers asked me to shotgun a beer with them after I told them a funny story (I declined). A trio of young women compared notes on which of their Tuesday-night hookups had the best dick. The son of a beer executive bragged about his father's millions before asking if he could do a line of cocaine off my center console (absolutely not). Couples kissed and groped each other in the backseat on the way to their apartments until I had to intervene before clothes started being removed. On every corner of the campus, intoxicated students stumbled through intersections and vomited in bushes. When I honked at a young man who was walking in the middle of the road, he flipped me off and challenged me to a fight before tripping over the curb and landing face-first on the sidewalk.

At least for the first week, students at FSU treated classes as an afterthought. At no point did I hear anyone discuss course-work. There were no pickups from the library, only trips to a drive-thru liquor store called Mike's Beer Barn to refill when the party ran dry. Flush from summer jobs and student loan cash, the students were determined to make their every dollar count by seeking out the cheapest drinks in town. Their constant movement fueled a bright red spot on my map for the entire week.

The relief that flooded me when I got home was indescribable. With the students back, my financial struggles disappeared like a late afternoon thunderstorm. The long working hours that had consumed me during the burning heat of the summer could finally come to an end. I told myself that I would cut back on my driving hours and take some days off, but the temptation to drive and earn was high. After barely surviving the summer months, a part of me burned to keep working in search of some vague concept of financial safety that could never really be achieved. My well-being was linked to putting in hours behind the wheel, and every moment of rest felt like a missed opportunity.

The strangest thing about the return of the students was the inversion that it created. During the summer, I had been forced to work more but have less. With my best customers back in town, I returned to a modest level of comfort. My grocery budget expanded again, and I never had to check my bank balance before washing my clothes. I was still living paycheck to paycheck, but I no longer teetered on the edge of financial collapse. If the promises of the gig economy had felt like a scam during the summer, the beginning of the school year felt like I was the one cheating the system. This wasn't bare survival. This was *making it*.

Driving continued to exhaust me, physically and emotionally, but there was a new opportunity on the horizon. I had signed up for Lyft as soon as it arrived in Tallahassee the year before, but it hadn't caught on right away. Sometime during the summer, Lyft began offering deeply discounted rides on their app, and as word spread, business on the platform picked up. On most nights, I would turn on both apps to scan for rides, logging off one when I was pinged on the other. In the event that I was pinged simultaneously, I would accept both and cancel the one that was further away. It gave me a little bit of choice in my work.

My permanent state of burnout had one unexpected benefit: I became immune to being manipulated by the apps. Each platform had unique ways of trying to earn my loyalty, but with my schedule fixed by my circumstances, their efforts were fruitless. I wasn't enticed by bonuses for driving during certain hours because my only option was to drive during *all* hours. The companies couldn't manipulate me, and because they couldn't, their attempts stuck out like a sore thumb.

Each platform introduced loyalty rewards to try to keep me driving, but none of the things on offer meant anything to me. Uber classified me as a Platinum driver, one level short of the Diamond tier occupied by full-time drivers. The marquee perk of the program was free tuition at Arizona State University online, a benefit that seemed laughable in light of my working hours. My fellow drivers and I worked endlessly and were paid so little that we could barely feed ourselves, yet we were somehow supposed to find the time to navigate registering for an online degree program. It felt more like an insult than a reward.

I was allowed to see the direction a trip would be headed before accepting it, as well as the estimated length of the ride. It was a privilege that the company gave to drivers in other states as a routine matter. In Florida, it was dangled as a perk for continued loyalty, one that could be revoked if I canceled too many rides or didn't accept 85 percent of the rides offered to me. Of course, it didn't matter which direction a rider wanted to go. I was going to accept the ride no matter what.

Lyft sent me a light-up bar that magnetically attached to my dashboard as a reward for my first few hundred rides. It glowed purple and helped riders spot my car in the dark. Neat, but ultimately just a gimmick. I was also given access to an "exclusive" online store where I could purchase hats and polo shirts embroidered with the company's logo, just in case I wanted to give some of my hard-earned money back to the people who barely saw fit to bestow it on me.

Amid all the discount oil changes and trip directions was an increase in the amount of messages that the apps sent me, some more obvious in their efforts to manipulate me than others. Rather than offering bonuses, Uber would send me notifications that a "quest" was available, as if giving twenty rides between Monday and Thursday was going to rescue a princess. The rewards for these quests were meager and in some cases amounted to little more than $0.50 per ride. On Friday nights, I would sometimes receive a message when I logged off to take a bathroom break: "By this time last week, you'd made more money than this. Don't you want to log back on and keep going?"

No amount of work was deemed enough by the apps. Lyft asked me to set a weekly goal and would push notifications to me if I was slower than the previous week in getting there. If I did hit the target, I'd be presented with a message encouraging me to keep going and see just how much I could earn. I began receiving a weekly progress report that showed how many five-star ratings I had received. Uber began making my driver rating much more prevalent in the interface and chastised me if the app detected me braking hard too frequently.

All of this has a name in tech circles: gamification, the process of making something like a game so that it snares the attention of the user. If you've ever been given a bonus item on a phone game just for opening the app, you've experienced this. The goal is to keep the app in your mind, to remind you of its presence, and to give you just a tiny hit of dopamine to keep you coming back. *Keep looking. Keep driving. You've been gone. We missed you. Don't you want to make some money?*

In rideshare, the gamification is multifaceted and nefarious. The earnings screen is not easily accessible during a ride, preventing you from seeing if you've hit your goal. When rides stack up one on top of the other, the apps give no opportunity to see what earnings you have. In the Lyft app, the default settings don't bother asking if you want to take another ride during your current ride; it simply plays a chime and accepts the ride for you, adding it on to the queue. Didn't want that one? Too bad. You didn't tell the app you didn't want it, and you wouldn't want to get in trouble for canceling it, would you?

Even if you do have a free moment between rides, the apps try to discourage you from looking at the earnings screen. In the Uber app, the info pane at the top of the map defaults to how many rides you've completed on your current quest. If there's no quest active, it shows your driver tier and how many points you've earned toward the next tier. Anything to avoid showing you the money, anything to trick you into staying online just a little bit longer. Anything for one more ride.

If all of this manipulation seems like it might leave drivers burned out, you're right, but the companies don't care. Uber and Lyft are concerned primarily with recruiting new drivers, not caring for existing ones. The immense amount of effort put into advertising the benefits of driving for the apps, the touting of sign-on bonuses and flexible hours and "being your own boss" are all there to hide the ugly little secret: turnover. Nearly every rideshare driver on the road has only been doing it for a few months. Almost universally, they will quit rather than continue to tolerate the low pay and uncertain opportunities. Just how bad is the "churn" of drivers? A study in 2017 determined that 97 percent of drivers quit within a year.[2]

By this point in my driving career, I had given thousands of rides. In rideshare terms, I was a dinosaur. My loyalty was guaranteed because the apps knew that if I could have done something else, I would have switched to doing it already. The companies had no incentive to cater to me, just as they had no incentive to cater to the thousands who had signed up after me. It didn't matter if drivers quit after a few months. By then, the apps had already taken their cut, and there would be more people signing up the next day. A handful of drivers signing up for online classes at a school in Arizona were paid for by the apps squeezing blood from a million different stones, and the companies know that there will always be a bigger fool willing to take the chance that, for them, it might be different.

Manipulation is the key to the gig economy's explosive growth, whether it takes the form of outright lies about earnings or subtler, more insidious "benefits." The gamified features of the apps are not a coincidence but the result of years of dedicated testing designed to determine the best way to keep drivers online.[3] The only way that Uber and other apps can keep wait times low is to make sure that a large pool of workers are sitting idle, waiting in reserve capacity to be assigned to a rider.

Between emails, texts, and app notifications, drivers are bombarded with messages pushing them to go online, and once they get there, the system works hard to keep them looking for the next ride. Earnings goals and reminders about how a driver earned more in a previous week are one way, but there are other, more creative methods. Assigning a driver the next ride before they've dropped off their current passenger is one way, as is the arbitrary way that apps award points and ranks (gold, diamond, platinum, etc.) for completing rides.

All of this is intentional, baked in from the beginning. Among Uber's first hires were a computational neuroscientist and a nuclear physicist, people who came from fields with backgrounds in experimentation and human behavior. As early as 2013, the company hired outside consultants to help find ways to manipulate drivers. Uber and other gig companies engage in this manipulation because the tremendous turnover of drivers on the platforms requires them to use the one resource they have in spades: information. The asymmetry between what the company knows about earnings and demand and what drivers are forced to guess leaves ample opportunity for it to exploit workers to its benefit. An online but idle driver benefits Uber but costs it nothing.

After I gave thousands of rides, the passengers began to blur together, one after another, day after day after day. It no longer amused me to see the highs and lows of the human experience, to witness the ways that people would share their darkest secrets and finest moments with a stranger.

It was difficult to remember when certain rides had happened, and I began to jot down stories in notepads, feeling that I would lose a part of myself if I forgot them. I eventually started a Twitter account where I began to catalog the people I met. I doubted that anyone would care about some Uber driver's day-to-day business, but there are blogs where people catalog their lunch every day. There's an audience for anything, even if it's just a few dozen people. Sharing my life online made me feel less alone, like I was leaving a record of my life (even if all I was really doing was screaming into the void).

The endless parade of humanity that shuffled through my car every night had come to define me. They were the most intimate connection in my life. My personal identity had blurred with the character I became while driving. The people who passed in and out of the backseat had become a part of me, and I owed my survival to them. I knew that they would not remember me, but if I forgot them, then I was a phantom, a ghost floating about town and silently bearing witness to the great spectrum of human experience. If the memories faded, I would disappear along with them.

When riders asked me for my wildest stories, I now had to ask them to clarify whether they wanted to hear a story that was funny or sad, disturbing or thrilling. I would change my answer to match the story to the mood of the car, hoping that if I could entertain or shock someone, I might be able to cajole them into tipping me just a few dollars (which had finally been incorporated as an option in the app). Every little bit helped.

Likewise, the college students no longer had the ability to shock me. For every time I'd been surprised by their behavior in the early days, I now had a dozen examples of the exact same circumstances. I could recognize someone who was chatty from someone who was coked up and someone who was on the verge of puking. On more than one occasion, I stopped at a stop sign, reached into the seat back, and handed the pre-opened trash bag to a student mere moments before their stomach rebelled at its liquid contents. I knew how to stand my ground against groups who wanted to squeeze extra passengers in the backseat, to lock the doors and refuse to let them in before they decided who to leave behind. They could dock my rating with a one-star review, but it didn't matter. There were hundreds of rides every month.

I jumped deftly between Uber and Lyft, focusing on whichever app could deliver rides the fastest. The college students were concentrated on Uber's platform, and when I tired of their antics or attitudes, I could switch to Lyft and find myself driving a much calmer crowd of locals. My ability to affect the flow of business was limited, but switching between apps let me have a small measure of influence over how I operated.

I couldn't control the prices the apps charged, nor could I control who I picked up, but I could try to spend my time in the most efficient way possible. With each app competing to attract drivers with varying bonuses and guarantees, I was able to take advantage of the platform that had the best promotions. Even on Friday nights, the prime time for price surges on Uber, I was sometimes able to pick up a big bonus for a single ride on Lyft. Picking up a ride worth $20 was well worth sitting in a parking lot for ten minutes until the app dinged.

Even the cleaning fees charged for making messes were open for manipulation. I learned from parking lot conversations with other drivers to always claim that a rider who had stuck their head out the window to vomit had gotten their mess in the window seals. That pushed the cleaning fee payment from $50 to $100. The key was to take lots of photos from different angles, a trick that made it seem like the vomit covered a much larger area. In reality, cleaning it up usually required a handful of paper towels and a bottle of water. Total time: five minutes, but by logging off of one app and working on the other while I waited for the cleaning fee, I could claim that the mess had taken ages to clean. Even if the material was only on the outside of the car, I was the one who had to clean up a stranger's puke. I would be compensated for the indignity of the entire affair even if it meant stretching the truth a little bit.

Time and struggle forged cynicism in my heart. Human beings were often stupid, brutish, and cruel. Not everyone was worth helping, and I learned to be reserved in my assistance. The endless nights behind the wheel expunged high-minded idealism from my soul. I could still talk and tell stories and laugh, but I found myself treating the people in my backseat as interchangeable mannequins. They were all just means to an end, yet they were still a defining part of me. My greatest sympathy and solidarity were reserved for the working poor, for the people who lived in the same scarcity-induced desperation that was my new normal.

I had become a robotic veteran of the gig economy, so used to working at every moment that I would sometimes lie down to sleep and find myself behind the wheel in my dreams. I had lasted far longer than most drivers, and my only reward was the ability to wake up the next day and do it all over again.

# CHAPTER 5

EVERY NIGHT BEHIND THE WHEEL HAD A PULSE, A MOOD THAT MIRRORED THE people in the backseat. Some nights were easygoing and joyous, while others were more somber, serious affairs. As the academic year wore on, I could tell the mood of the students by the way they climbed into the backseat and milled about on the sidewalks. The worst nights were filled with angry tension, blanketed in a fog of aggression.

The Friday night I met Ophelia was one such night. From the moment I logged on, every carload of students had been argumentative and hostile. I had spent the night telling students no. *No, you can't bring your beer in the car. No, you can't fit six people in my backseat. No, I'm not going to make an exception.* By the time Ophelia sat down in my passenger seat, I was annoyed, tired, and ready for a break.

Ophelia and her friends were drunk, but that wasn't unusual. A mixed group of college students, they were leaving happy hour and ready to move on to the next part of their night. From outside the car, I could hear the voices of several young men asking where the group was going and whether they were going to ride together. Such conversations were fairly common, and I steeled myself to once again explain that I wasn't going to allow more people in my backseat than it had seatbelts for. From outside the car, I heard a voice say that there wasn't enough room in the car for everyone, and another voice replied that there was always room in the trunk. I groaned in frustration as the back hatch of my SUV popped open and the car sank with the weight of bodies piling into the back. Not for the first time, I unbuckled my seatbelt and got out to explain that no one was going to be riding alongside my son's car seat.

I rounded the back of the car to see a trio of young men sitting in the rear of the vehicle, attempting to fit themselves among the various objects I kept in my trunk. There, flushed red with alcohol and shirtless, was where I encountered Zachary Tyler Burnette.

"No one is riding in the back," I said firmly. "You guys need to get out."

"It's fine. We can fit," Burnette replied.

"No one is riding in the back," I repeated. The other men looked at each other uneasily and began climbing out of the trunk. Their opening the back hatch felt like a ludicrous invasion of my privacy, because the area where I kept my son's car seat and toys was private. I thought of it as off-limits, and any time a passenger opened the back hatch, it made me want to turn them away on principle. This little stunt had made me angry, and I resolved that none of these men were getting a ride from me. I turned to look at the last man in the back, Burnette.

"Get out of my car," I repeated.

"No," Burnette said.

"Get the fuck out of my car!" I yelled, reaching into the back to take Burnette by the arm and tug him toward the street where his friends were already gathering.

Big mistake.

The moment I touched him, Burnette lunged, wrapping me up and pushing me backward. My heels caught the edge of the curb as I stepped back, and I tumbled onto the sidewalk. Burnette landed on top of me, knocking every bit of air in my chest out of me. I gasped for air as he grabbed me by the hair and slammed my head into the pavement. I tried desperately to push him off of me but succeeded only in wiggling around on the concrete.

As Burnette slammed my head into the ground again, a strange clarity fell over me: this should hurt, and the fact that it didn't was a bad sign. Unable to push him off me, I pulled myself toward my attacker, thinking that if he couldn't push me down, he couldn't beat me to death against the pavement. My attempt was only partially successful. Burnette slammed my back into the ground again before seizing me by the top of the head, leaning back, and lining up a perfect right hand with my left eye.

The punch drove my head into the pavement so hard that my skull bounced off the ground. Things got a little fuzzy after that. I remember hearing a woman screaming. I remember a few more punches. I remember having enough clarity to realize that I was about to die, beaten to death by a student on the dirty ground outside of a college bar. As I waited for the blow that I assumed would end me, I felt an insane urge to laugh. Finally, I could rest. Finally, all of my struggling would be over.

The deathblow never came. From somewhere beyond my hazy consciousness, someone pushed Burnette off of me. I rolled onto my knees and gasped for air. Someone grabbed my hand and helped me to stand up. Ophelia, looking shocked, handed me my glasses. They had come off in the initial fall backward onto the pavement. I looked about desperately, trying to determine if

I was still in danger. A crowd of college students had surrounded the scene.

"That was on you, homie," one of Ophelia's male friends sneered at me. I turned and ran to my car to grab my phone. I frantically dialed 911 as I began closing the now empty back hatch of my car. One of Ophelia's friends opened a passenger door, saying something about retrieving a phone from the car. I yelled that he could have his phone when the police got here, grabbing him by the waist and yanking him out of the backseat. One by one, I closed the doors and locked them, wondering why the emergency operator wasn't talking to me.[1] By the time it dawned on me that my phone was still connected to the car's Bluetooth, 911 had already hung up and started trying to call me back.

I opened the driver's side door and climbed inside to talk to the operator. Locking the doors, I explained that I had just been attacked by a passenger, did not know if I was still in danger, and needed officers on the scene immediately. The dispatcher was kind, calm, and professional. She stayed on the line with me until the cops rolled up. By the time blue lights mounted the curb behind me, the crowd of students had dissipated. Ophelia and her friends were gone. Burnette was nowhere to be found.

I was barely able to tell the officers what had happened. The time between getting out of my car and having my head slammed into the pavement might have been thirty seconds. When the officers asked me to describe my assailant, my memory failed entirely. I remembered a tattoo because he had been shirtless, but every other detail was blank. The officers rolled their eyes at the idea of searching for a suspect described only as a shirtless white male with an unknown tattoo but dutifully jotted down the description. As I struggled to recall the details, an ambulance arrived. The EMTs pulled me away from the officers to evaluate my condition. After shining a light in my eyes and asking me some questions, they recommended that I go to the hospital. I thought about my car, parked on the side of the road in the middle of a busy college area. It would be towed within a few hours, and I had no money to get it out of an impound lot. It was the beginning of the month, and my bank account was nearly empty. I told the medics that I would drive myself.

•   •   •

When I got out of the ambulance, the police were talking to a group of Kuwaiti exchange students. One of the men had seen the altercation from the beginning and was giving a description of Burnette to the officers. Thinking quickly, one member of the group had recorded most of the incident on his phone. I wrote down a statement and let the officers take pictures of my battered face. The Kuwaitis showed me the video they had taken of my encounter. I would love to tell you that it showed me admirably defending myself, that I went blow for blow and held my ground. That would be a lie. The video shows a helpless man on his back being pummeled into the concrete.

With the reports filed and pictures taken, the officers departed. I climbed back into the driver's seat and started the car, unsure of what to do. I took a few moments to report the incident to Uber, unsure of what would come from telling the company that part of my rider's entourage had tried to kill me. Pulling away into the night, I found myself being drawn toward a liquor store. The clerks did a double take when I walked in the door and immediately asked if I was alright. I mumbled something about having been in a fight and grabbed a bottle of bourbon.

The clerk joked that he'd hate to see the other guy. I drove back to my apartment and poured straight bourbon into a glass. With a deep breath, I walked into the bathroom to take a look at myself for the first time.

The man in the mirror was a mess. No wonder the liquor store clerks had been so concerned. My left eye was swollen, and a deep, black bruise had already emerged around the socket. My face had a line of blood down one side, the remnant of a cut on my scalp. I ran my hand across my head and came away with a bloody clump of matted hair. I washed my face and stared at the glass of bourbon, wanting it but knowing that it wouldn't really help me. I was bruised, bloody, and alone. There was one person I could call, but I doubted that she would even talk to me.

Marie didn't answer the first call. Or the second. Or the third. By the time I decided to call a fourth time, I was beginning to feel foolish. It was long past the time that she would have been in bed, and the voice that finally picked up on the other end was clearly sleepy. As soon as she heard my voice, she knew something bad had happened. In rambling words punctuated by occasional sobs, the story poured out of me. I told her that I felt guilty, as if I'd brought the violence on myself. She reassured me that I was the victim and urged me to go to the hospital to get checked out.

I paused, unsure of what to say. I didn't want to admit to Marie that I was too poor to afford the emergency room. Even before the liquor store, I didn't have the money for my co-pay. I only had $77 in my bank account, and that was before I'd wasted money on alcohol. I finally told her that all I wanted was to take a shower and go to bed. Marie pressed me. If I wasn't going to go to the hospital, I should at least come over to the house and sleep there so that she could keep an eye on me. I declined and reiterated that I was just going to take a shower and go to bed. She made me promise to call in the morning before hanging up.

I set the bourbon on the bathroom sink and turned on the shower. Stepping under the water showed me even more of my injuries. Clumps of hair ran off my head, and the warm water reopened a cut on my head that turned the shower floor pink with blood. My back burned with a thousand tiny cuts caused by being ground into the rough pavement. I stepped out of the shower and looked at the glass sitting by the sink. For all I knew, I was bleeding into my skull, risking the type of injury that meant I would go to sleep and never wake up. I poured the liquor down the drain and went to bed.

■ ■ ■

When I (luckily) woke up the next morning, I had two missed calls. The first, from Marie, was to check on me. I called her back and let her know I hadn't died overnight. We planned how to explain my appearance to Alex in a way that wouldn't scare him. Dad had been working as the Taxi Man, and there was a bad man who hit me. The police were helping, but Dad might need some time to recover and might not be able to play as much as usual. It was simple, direct, and covered all the issues without leaving too much room for Alex's imagination to run wild.

The second call was from Uber's support line. I made myself a cup of instant coffee and called back. The man who answered was confused about why I was calling. When I explained that I was a driver who had been attacked by a passenger, he gave me a cursory apology and ran through a short checklist of questions. Did I have dashcam footage of the incident? Was there a police report? Was I currently safe? The last question made me snort. I was standing in my kitchen. It had been ten hours since the en-counter. The entire sequence of questions was not meant to help me but to help Uber evaluate its liability. Uber wasn't concerned with me. Rather, its concern was how much of a corporate head-ache would result from my near-death experience. The call ended with a commitment that Uber would "thoroughly investigate" the incident. There was no compensation for my injuries, no offer to cover a trip to the emergency room. I wasn't dead, and that was all Uber cared about.

In any other job, my employer would have been responsible for covering the costs of my treatment. At the very least, the company would have paid for the initial assessment at the ER to determine the extent of my wounds. Businesses carry liability insurance for just this reason. If you employ someone, you're expected to care for their safety and well-being while they're on the job. You can't just dump them on the street and wash your hands of them the second they become an inconvenience (unless you're a gig company).

Sipping my coffee, I opened up the driver app and looked at my earnings. With a sinking feeling, I realized I was well short of my weekly goal. I had come to rely on the money I made by working long hours on Friday night, particularly on the weekends when I was scheduled to spend Sunday with Alex. Since my night had been cut short, I was nearly $100 away from my goal. Especially at the beginning of the month, missing out on that money meant losing out on basic necessities.

Gutted, I tried to reassure myself with brave thoughts. I was a strong, experienced driver who'd had a bad incident. Normally, I felt safe and powerful behind the wheel. This was my livelihood, and I wasn't going to let some violent drunk take my power away from me. I had chosen this life with the knowledge that there would be bad times, and while this was worse than I had ever imagined, I soothed my anxiety by reminding myself why I was working so hard.

All of this was an attempt to rationalize away my real feelings: I had been brutally assaulted, and I had no idea what the long-term effects of that would be. I didn't want to get back in my car. I had no desire to pick up load after load of strangers and ferry them about town. I wanted to lie down, to sleep, and to recover. I raged at the unfairness of my life, that I could work two jobs and still be forced to go back to work the day after a near-death experience, but all of my rage was ultimately pointless. The money needed to be made, and there was only one way to get it. My stomach wrenched at the realization that I had no choice. I had to go back out. With the instant coffee burning a hole in my stomach, I grabbed an old baseball cap to cover my black eye and headed for the car.

. . .

Monday morning at work was disastrous. Despite calling my boss ahead of time to warn her that something bad had happened over the weekend, I was forced to repeat the story of my assault to every curious coworker I bumped into in the hallway. Between my boss, old coworkers, and a well-meaning special agent supervisor, at least a half dozen times in the first few hours at the office, I relived being assaulted.

Worse, I was increasingly aware of a strange defect in my vision. What had started on Saturday had only worsened during my Sunday with Alex, and by Monday, I could no longer ignore it. Whenever I turned my head too quickly, I was briefly blinded by a flash of light in my left eye. I had told myself I was imagining things while driving on Saturday, that I was catching a street light or a reflection out of the corner of my eye. On Sunday, my denial deepened to insist that I was imagining things, but by Monday, I'd had enough time to experiment with turning my head at different speeds to realize that something was very wrong. Stepping into the break room, I called a local eye doctor's office and asked if they could bill me later for an emergency appointment. To my great relief, they agreed. I explained the situation to my boss and left to be examined.

The eye doctor was young, fresh out of medical residency, and deeply sympathetic to my situation. Still, I was once again forced to explain exactly what had happened. After an initial examination, she put drops into my eyes and began a series of tests involving a set of glass lenses that she pulled from a monogrammed box. Her conclusions were not reassuring.

"Your eyes haven't been damaged," she told me, "but there's a risk of future damage. The fluid inside your eye is usually thick, like a gel. The impacts have liquefied some of this, and whenever your head moves, the fluid is sloshing around inside your eye."

She explained that the flashes of light were caused by the optic nerve being tugged as the fluid moved around. I asked her if the damage was permanent. She told me that my eye would probably recover.

"Probably?" I asked.

"Either that," she said, "or you'll go blind."

I asked if there was anything I could do to help the healing process, but she told me that there was no way of knowing what would happen. If I didn't go blind within a few weeks, I would probably recover after three months. I struggled to maintain my composure as she put the lenses away. All I had wanted was to make sure that everyone in my car would be safe, that I would have a seatbelt for everyone, and now I had to live with the fear that every time I turned my head to look at something, it might be the last thing I would ever see.

I left the office and sat down behind the wheel of my car, grateful for a sunny day that gave me an excuse to hide my black eye behind my sunglasses. I texted my boss that I had gotten bad news and was taking the rest of the day off. Then I turned on the app and got back to surviving.

The situation with the police left me with little hope. A detective that contacted me after the incident called me in to do a photo lineup, but with very little idea of what my attacker actually looked like, I struggled to choose a photo from the series that she presented to me. Feeling pressured to do something, I picked a photo and wrote on the back that I was only partially sure that the person in the photo was my attacker. When I exited the interview room, I asked the detective if I had chosen the right photo. She shook her head and told me that it was unlikely the state attorney would file charges against my assailant.

The girl who had called the ride had told police her side of the story, as had a number of bystanders. Somehow, officers had made a positive ID on Burnette. After he left me in a bloody pile, his friends had stopped him from returning to finish me off, at which point he had stormed into a nearby fraternity house, kicked a hole in the wall, and fled into the night. I was shocked to learn that my assailant was not a college student but a grown man in his mid-twenties from Gainesville. Out for a night on the town in Tallahassee's wild party scene, he had come into a town, beaten a stranger half to death, and then gone back to his job at a car dealership.

The knowledge that Burnette wasn't from Tallahassee helped me. I had spent several weeks calling every rider named "Zachary" before picking them up to grill them about their last name, a conversation that always resulted in questions about why. The questions meant I had to explain myself, and that meant reliving the assault again and again. At work and in the car, I was telling the story of what had happened on a daily basis. The mental strain was constant. I began to have nightmares of a dark figure above me, raising his fist as I squirmed helplessly. Sometimes the dream would last for what felt like an eternity as I struggled to crawl away. When the blow eventually came from the shadow phantom, I would wake up screaming.

Daytime was no better. My moods would shift randomly and without reason, leaving me confused and disoriented. In one incident, I was drinking water in my kitchen when my hand spasmed and dropped the glass, sending sharp fragments everywhere. I found myself consumed with rage, a burning desire to throw things and beat my fists against the walls. I screamed in fury before bursting into confused tears, suddenly so despondent that I could scarcely breathe.

Still without medical guidance, I received a few answers from a doctor who called a ride because her car was in the shop. When I described my symptoms, she told me in no uncertain terms that I was experiencing the aftermath of a severe concussion and urged me to take time off to let my eye and my brain heal. I didn't have the heart to tell her that her solution wasn't an option.

. . .

The court case for the man who assaulted me took years to re-solve. As I worked late nights and long hours, I would sometimes come home to find a letter in my mailbox from the prosecutor's office notifying me of various actions being taken. As the victim, I was entitled to be notified of every change in the case, and every motion and rescheduled hearing left me a wreck. Each time I spotted an envelope in my mailbox, my anxiety would overwhelm me. Each one was a reminder of one of the worst nights of my life, and I came to dread opening them.

The letters were meant to inform me of upcoming hearings. I had no ability to control the outcome of the process, but I was determined to attend every hearing, to be an active advocate for whatever little piece of justice I could get. For each one, I would dutifully add the date to my calendar and request time off from work. The day before, I would contact the prosecutor's office to find out if things were still on schedule. The hearings never happened. As the months passed, I received letter after letter notifying me of the date and time for the next hearing. Inevitably, my attacker's lawyer would request an extension or reschedule. At some point, he fired his first lawyer and hired a second one. The second lawyer also requested extensions.

Between the hearings, I did my best to forget that they were happening. I had to focus on my immediate needs and trust that the wheels of justice would keep turning even if I took my eyes off them. I worked in law enforcement and knew that things in-volving the courts often took ages to sort out. The best revenge against my assailant was to keep living my life as if nothing had

happened. I wasn't going to let that night stop me from doing
what needed to be done.

My case, a misdemeanor assault, was a low priority for the
state attorney's office, one that normally would not have even
merited much attention. I was lucky that any charges were
brought at all. I had failed to identify my attacker in a lineup,
and if the woman who called the ride hadn't come forward to
offer details, the case would never have advanced.

I pursued the prosecutor's office on a regular basis, tracking
the case as it was handed from one junior attorney to another.
Turnover in the office was high, and I found myself repeating
the details for each prosecutor assigned to the case. Some of the
attorneys were comforting and took an interest in the incident.
Others tried to tell me not to expect much even as they did very
little to advance the case. One particularly active prosecutor took
the time to review the evidence and told me it was a slam dunk.

"This Burnette guy is on video attacking you. If he goes to
trial, he's an idiot," he told me just a few weeks before being
assigned to other, more important cases.

I wrote a lengthy victim impact statement for the court. I
detailed the various physical, mental, and emotional issues I had
suffered since the attack. I wrote about constant anxiety, panic
attacks, and nightmares. I detailed the slow recovery of my vision
and the concussion symptoms I had experienced. I wrote about
my experience during the attack and my belief that if someone
had not pushed him off of me, Burnette would gladly have beaten
me to death. I closed by asking for the court to assess the maxi-
mum penalty for the attack, a paltry year in jail.

The letter was met with approval by the prosecutors who
read it, but they mostly scoffed at my request for jail time. As

they tried to temper my expectations, the prosecutors made it clear that they found it unlikely my assailant would spend even a single day in jail. The assault that had left me a bloody heap on the nighttime pavement was his first offense. One attorney told me that their office planned to request a few months of probation, as well as alcohol and anger management counseling. I told them that was unacceptable.

Sitting at my desk in my cramped, gray-walled cubicle, I cried and told the prosecutor how I'd had to explain what happened to my son, to my coworkers, and to so many of my passengers. I'd been forced to relive the moment hundreds of times, and each time had been a repetition of the trauma of the event. There had been a period of several months where I was unsure if I was going to go blind in one eye. I talked about the bizarre desire to laugh during the attack as I thought that I was about to die on the grimy pavement. No, I said, probation wasn't going to cut it. The young woman on the other end of the line stayed quiet for a long time before telling me that she would rewrite the plea offer. The best she could offer was six weeks in jail, and even that was unlikely. I thanked her for being willing to try and hung up to have a panic attack.

. . .

Months later, at the beginning of 2020, I received a call from the state attorney's office while I was at work. The new prosecutor assigned to the case had decided it had been sitting on the docket long enough: it was time for this misdemeanor assault case to be resolved. She talked through the case with me and let me know that Burnette's attorney had indicated he wanted to take the case to trial. Was I willing to testify?

Absolutely, I said.

She warned me that the judge assigned was known to be lenient with first-time offenders. Burnette's lawyer likely intended for him to plead guilty and beg the judge for mercy. The plea deal was too harsh, and a guilty plea was likely to result in a lesser sentence than the state's office had offered. He might even receive only a fine.

She asked if we could discuss a different plea deal, one that would involve an option besides incarceration. Rather than being locked up, Burnette would be allowed to serve a shorter sentence at a work camp, an option she described as "daytime jail." He would spend his days picking up trash in the Florida sun and be allowed to go home at night. Rather than six weeks, she thought twenty-five days sounded like a good replacement. The other punishments (alcohol monitoring, counseling, etc.) would stand.

I told the prosecutor that I needed some time to think about it and asked if I could call her back. Nearly two years of letters, calls, and hearing notices had left me emotionally exhausted. As I slouched in my chair, a supervisor stopped by and asked me to step into their office. They closed the door behind us and proceeded to lay into me for pursuing "personal matters" during work time.

Humiliated and frustrated, I told them that things were coming to a close, that we would be going to trial. They told me that it needed to be over, that I'd been spending far too much time talking to the prosecutor's office over such a minor matter. When I protested that someone nearly beating me to death was not a "minor matter," they told me that I'd had a black eye and should stop exaggerating. I sat in stony silence as they finished chewing me out.

When I got back to my desk, I called the prosecutor back. The deal was fine, I told her. She said she'd call Burnette's lawyer and make the offer. A half hour later, my phone rang again. Burnette's lawyer was going to take the case to trial and Burnette would plead guilty. I told her to call Burnette's lawyer back and tell him that I would pass on suing him in civil court if he would take the deal. She said she would run it past him to see if it would help.

It did.

On January 23, 2020, more than twenty months after he assaulted me, Zachary Tyler Burnette pled no contest to one count of misdemeanor battery and was sentenced to a year of probation, twenty-four days in a jail work camp, and anger management and alcohol abuse classes.[2] He was ordered to pay me $77 in restitution, the cost of my emergency eye doctor visit. In addition to whatever he paid his lawyer, he paid almost $800 in court costs.

He will live the rest of his life with a conviction for a violent crime on his record. I do not know why the prosecutor's office told me twenty-five days in a jail work camp but sought only twenty-four days on the final paperwork. Justice works in strange ways, and I tell myself that this is justice. Mostly, I am glad that the entire ordeal is over. After that initial phone call the day after the assault, I never heard another word from Uber about the assault. There was no compensation for my injuries, no checkup on my well-being.

Perhaps I'd have been less surprised by the lack of response if I had known more about the company's history. All across the world, Uber has expressed concern for driver well-being in press releases, but its actions tell a different story. In the company's initial growth phases, it was common for drivers to have altercations with taxi drivers upset at the app's disruption of their livelihoods.

Rather than take steps to protect the people fueling their company's growth, Uber employees kept close track of violent confrontations between cab drivers and gig workers across Europe and used the violence as fuel for public relations. When taxi drivers in the Netherlands began attacking Uber drivers with hammers and brass knuckles in March 2015, Uber told the drivers to file police reports, which were surreptitiously leaked to the press. One Uber manager bragged to leadership that the story would be on the front page of one of the country's largest newspapers "without our fingerprint." Uber leveraged the bloody incidents to win meetings with government officials where it could pitch them on allowing the company to operate outside of regulations.[3]

The lack of concern for driver safety was even worse in South Africa, where Uber implemented a program to allow riders to pay drivers in cash. Internal discussions showed that the company knew that it was putting drivers at risk of being robbed but implemented the program anyway. Local gangs took advantage of the policy to rob and kidnap drivers, and in some cases, drivers were murdered. When drivers protested outside Uber's corporate office, the company ignored them.[4] The message was clear: safety isn't a concern.

CHAPTER **6**

TAD AND HIS FRIENDS DIDN'T SEEM THAT UNUSUAL WHEN I FIRST SAW THEM walking toward the car. The foursome looked like every other carload of frat boys I'd picked up that night, but their trip had a bigger purpose than just getting drunk. While the first trip to the car came with two cases of beer and a grocery bag full of snacks, they made me wait as they ran back inside to get more party supplies. Along with more beer came a laptop, a projector, and a portable projection screen. As I started the ride and put the car in gear, my curiosity overwhelmed me.

"Big plans tonight?" I asked as an opener. The four young men all started talking simultaneously. After a brief moment of confusion, Tad took charge of responding.

"Oh yeah, bro," he started, "we're staging an intervention for our friend." My mind swirled with possibilities about what might be going on. The hard-drinking students of FSU could surely use some intervention when it came to alcohol, but with several cases of beer in tow, it didn't make sense to confront their friend about his drinking while bringing more alcohol along. I told Tad I was sorry to hear about his friend and asked what was going on. Maybe he had developed a drug problem? Cocaine use among the college students was disturbingly common (especially among the fraternities). It seemed like a strong possibility. Tad leaned forward from the backseat.

"It's our friend, bro. He's dating this girl, and bro, she's so terrible." Tad's friends murmured bro-laden confirmations, beginning and ending most of their sentences with the word.

"She's awful. She's really mean and controlling. She doesn't let him go out anymore, and bro, she's not even that hot. Like, he could do way better." The bros murmured their agreement.

"Okay," I said, "but that doesn't explain the projector . . ."

All four of the young men began talking excitedly. My car briefly became a cacophony of excited bro-ing.

"We made a PowerPoint, bro. He's getting a whole presentation," Tad said, beaming.

"It's *seven slides*, bro," another of the young men interjected. "*Seven slides.*" He said it with the sort of pride that one would usually reserve for describing a newborn child, not a minimal slideshow presentation. I wondered if he was including a title slide in the count. Tad cut in again.

"Bro, we even put in a whole slide on how all the other girls he used to go out with were way hotter." His friends murmured their agreement.

Navigating through traffic, I stifled the urge to laugh at the absurdity. These four kids were so upset with their friend's choice of companion that they were planning to ambush him with a full-scale presentation on her perceived inadequacy. I wondered how the lady in question would feel about being the subject of such a targeted intervention.

"You're going to give him the presentation, and then what?" I asked. With their destination approaching, I had to know Tad's endgame.

"Easy, bro. We're going to convince him to call her and break up. Then, we're gonna throw a party. We even have a couple of bitches ready to come over afterward." Tad's friends laughed and commended themselves for their ingenuity. They were going to rescue their friend from the tyranny of this woman and deliver him into the arms of salvation. I pulled into the parking lot of the apartment complex that was their destination and wished Tad and his friends good luck. As they unloaded their supplies, Tad thanked me for the ride and reiterated his confidence in their plan. Carrying their supplies, the four men left me alone in my car to laugh at their certainty.

As my phone dinged with another nearby ride, I wondered not about Tad and his slideshow but the unnamed friend. These frat boys were concerned enough to reach out and try to help, an act of outreach that felt alien to me. Winding through the drunken chaos of the night, I was struck by my solitude. I did not have anyone to intervene in my life. There was no group of friends waiting back at my apartment to rescue me from myself, no brothers who would care about my well-being. The only person who could care enough to try to make my life better was me.

■　■　■

I opened up a spreadsheet one day at work to do some quick math to determine what my hourly wage as a driver had been the previous year. Uber had made all sorts of promises about the hourly rates of drivers, with some ads saying that drivers made more than $19 per hour.[1] My experience was quite different. Even considering the constant business that the students brought me, my earnings were nowhere near the pie-in-the-sky promises of the app company's propaganda. Driving for twenty hours per week, I was making a little less than $15 per hour before factoring in all the gas I burned. I wasn't sure how to calculate my expenses, but I knew that frequent oil changes factored in. There was some sort of formula for depreciation I'd seen mentioned on tax forms, but I didn't know how to calculate it. I guessed that my real income was about $10–$12 per hour. It was more than I had been making at the game store in the mall, but not by much. My desire for flexibility had driven me to believe that I could beat the odds in a college town. Instead, I was spending my every waking hour worrying about finding enough rides to survive.

I wasn't alone in this disconnect. Uber had advertised that drivers working full-time in top markets made as much as $90,000 per year, but most drivers make far less.[2] All across the United States, rideshare drivers who shared their income statements with the online portal Ridester reported incomes far below the estimates that came from the app companies. The hourly rate reported by drivers was $14.73.[3] Most studies estimate that drivers have $4–$5 of expenses per hour in fuel and maintenance costs, so the real rate for the work is a little over $9 per hour. Uber's advertising about driver pay was so misleading that the Federal Trade Commission fined the company $20 million in 2017.[4]

As much as I liked the flexibility of being able to choose my own hours, there was very little value if the hours I had to work could be summarized as "every waking moment." I closed the spreadsheet where I had been calculating my expenses and hourly rates. It wasn't that I was doing any worse than other drivers, for we had all been victimized by the apps and their slick marketing. We lived by the algorithm's mercy, but the companies that ruled our existence had suckered us into the work with big promises that weren't panning out for anyone. We were supposed to be our own bosses, choose our own hours, and work only when we wanted. None of those statements were true, and in their place was a system that left us to sacrifice our dignity and well-being just to scrape by.

There comes a point in poverty when you become keenly aware that you aren't going to make it. Whether it's the weighty knowledge that you can't afford a trip to the grocery store, that you can't afford gas, or that you must pick a bill that will go unpaid, there is always a realization that you've done everything within your power but are still going to lose. Even when you cut back, you know in the back of your mind that there is a limit to how much you can do without. No amount of hustle or hard work can save you when you fall behind if you are already maxed out on sacrifices. The only option is to take desperate measures, to find a way to cheat the system by cutting corners or amputating a piece of yourself so that the rest of you can survive. You bargain with your own stomach about whether a peanut butter sandwich counts as dinner or whether breakfast is *really* as important as you were taught as a child.

My breaking point came one May as the students departed. Even with all the hours I was working, I looked at my budget and realized that I wasn't going to be able to pay my rent at the end of the month. My gas expenses were way up from hours spent tooling aimlessly around town hunting for rides, but my income was stagnant. The locals just didn't call rides like the college kids, and no amount of extra hours could make up for a lack of demand. I had gone from driving four to five days per week to every day. I spent every night and every weekend behind the wheel, sacrificing sleep to find more hours where I could drive. It wasn't working.

With the way the month was going, I would be a little less than $200 short by the time the rent was due. My desire to hide my situation from my parents excluded them from any possible requests for assistance. I was too ashamed to ask for help, but I could find no good options. What hurt the most was that I wasn't *that* far away from being able to pay my bills. If I had anything of value, I could have sold it for the money to survive. There were no good options anymore. The gap was too big to make up in a single jump. I needed something that would give me a better return than driving, something that I could do on top of everything that I was already doing.

I racked my brain at work for ways that I could make extra money. What little time off I had earned needed to be saved for emergencies, but surely this qualified. I considered calling in sick for a few days so that I could spend them driving, but even that wouldn't save me. The extra gas I would burn meant that I needed to make even more money. The more I drove, the more expenses I would have. I'd faced this hurdle before, but it had never been this high.

The solution came from a passenger who didn't say a word. She emerged from the double doors of a nondescript stall in a strip mall looking exhausted. She climbed in and went home, but it was the bandage on her arm that led me to investigate the place she had come from.

The following Sunday, I woke up early and made my first visit to the Biomat plasma center. The dim lighting, gruff staff, and dingy linoleum flooring didn't deter me. The place reeked of antiseptic and desperation, but it promised salvation. The entire experience was dehumanizing, meant to streamline human beings into an industrial product. In that way, it wasn't so different from gig work. Glossy posters on the walls advertised that I was giving "the gift of life," but the only person I was saving was myself. Printed notices taped to the doors touted that donors could make $400 if they donated eight times in a month.

I sat through an informational video about donating plasma that explained how it was different from donating blood, that the watery portion of my blood would be separated for use in advanced medicines used to treat rare cancers and hemophilia. A nurse gave me a cursory physical and told me to drink plenty of water before my next visit. After that, I was called back to a room with row after row of beds where a large needle went into my arm. I squeezed a squishy blue football stamped with the company's logo while the machine drew out my blood, spun it in a centrifuge, and pumped some of it back into me. The rest was dripped into a plastic bottle until I had reached the 875-milliliter mark. I looked around the room during the hour it took to give my first donation, recognizing several former passengers.

There were people in the uniforms of car dealerships and fast-food restaurants. In the corner, a man in dirty boots talked loudly about his job in construction to another man in paint-splattered overalls. A few young people played on their phones with one hand. I wanted to tell myself that these people were donating out of the goodness of their hearts, that they wanted to be part of a life-saving process, but I knew the real reason. We were all in that sterile, fluorescent-lit factory of human suffering for the same reason. Our common denominator was that despite our best efforts, we couldn't make ends meet, and this was a legal way of selling our bodies in order to squeeze out just a little bit more.

When it was done, I walked weakly out of the center with a bandage on my arm and an envelope containing my cash card.

After my first two donations, I would be given $150. With just one more donation, I could make it through the month. I sat in my car and cried from the shame of what I had been reduced to, a man so desperate that I could only pay my bills in blood money. When the sadness faded, I dried my eyes, turned on the app, and got to work.

.   .   .

Samantha and Max called for a ride to go home from the bar around midnight. A heavyset couple, they stumbled toward the car in obvious impairment. Max climbed in the backseat while Samantha asked if she could sit up front. On my guard, I agreed. Couples that sat separately had usually been arguing, and I decided that the best way to handle this pair was to keep my mouth shut and get them home quickly. Once I swiped to start the ride, I knew my plan wasn't going to work. Samantha's house was on the outskirts of town, almost a half hour away. I was going to be stuck with these two for a long time.

From the start, Samantha was chatty, asking about my night, the age of my car, and whether I enjoyed driving. I gave short, noncommittal answers and tried to focus on the road. Samantha asked me where I was from, and I gave her my standard answer. From the backseat, Max began to grumble. Samantha told me to ignore him and clarified without prompting that they were just friends, not a couple.

"Not this bullshit again. You always do this," Max mumbled. Samantha told him to hush and continued peppering me with questions. When Max interrupted, she told him to be quiet and apologized to me. Samantha explained that Max could be an angry drunk, but her apology only put me further on guard. The memory of being attacked was still fresh, and I had no interest in conflict with another passenger. As we moved through the night, Max began asking how much longer the ride would take. In the most reassuring tone I could manage, I told him we would be there soon. We were only a few blocks away from turning onto the highway when Max began pulling on the door handle.

"I can't take this shit anymore. I'm out of here," he said. I quickly tried to reassure him that we would be at their destination soon. He could close his eyes and relax. We'd be there in no time. We stopped at a red light near the highway entrance as Max drunkenly tried to figure out the door handle.

"No, fuck this. I'm out," Max declared. I felt something hit me in the face as the door opened. My fight-or-flight reflex leapt into action, pumping me full of adrenaline and slowing down my perception of time. I shifted the car into park and whirled around, hands up as I tried to determine whether I was in danger again. Max stumbled out of the car, ran across the empty lanes of traffic, and disappeared into the night. Panicked, I groped in the dark car to try to determine what had just been thrown at me. Samantha rolled down the window and yelled for Max to come back. I locked the doors and quickly gathered the unknown projectiles.

In the dim glow of the streetlights, I was able to make out what Max had thrown at me: three folded $20 bills. I quickly stuffed them in my pocket and briefly wondered if this was what being a stripper felt like. Samantha gave up trying to convince Max to get back in the car. I asked if we should turn around and try to look for him, but every part of me hoped she would say no.

"He'll find his own way home," she said. It was her account that had called the ride, and I told her she was the boss. She told me this wasn't the first time that Max had caused a scene while intoxicated. Although she insisted they weren't together, she said he would get jealous and angry when he'd been drinking. She'd learned to live with it, to let him have his tantrums. We pulled onto the highway, and Samantha resumed questioning me about my life. I gritted my teeth as the adrenaline rush ended and sweat poured out of me, trying to answer her politely even as I felt the urge to grind my teeth until my jaw ached. I eventually relaxed and made small talk. With Max out of the vehicle, I was more forthcoming in my answers, and by the time we arrived at her house, I had begun to enjoy chatting with Samantha. Sitting in her driveway, she apologized yet again for Max's behavior and asked if she could make it up to me.

"You're a good-looking guy. Maybe you could come inside for a drink? I can make it worth your while . . ." she told me, letting her fingers run along my arm. I was unused to being hit on like this, so it took a moment for what she was offering to sink in. I thought of myself as unattractive and unlovable, and the idea that anyone would find me desirable was difficult to process. My mind reeled as I wondered how often women drivers had to deal with things like this. I was alone in the driveway of a stranger's house in the middle of the night. Nothing about this environment felt safe.

I thanked her for the offer and told her it was very flattering, but I needed to get back to work. Embarrassed at being rejected, Samantha said goodbye and gathered her things. For all I knew, Max would be showing up in another car just a few minutes behind us. Maybe the whole incident had been planned, and I was the unwitting pawn. It was seedy, uncomfortable, and suspicious. The last thing I needed was to be fodder for a tabloid news story: "Uber Driver Killed in Domestic Dispute." I could see the headline in my mind's eye, complete with a sad obituary stating that I left behind a young son. There were a lot of things missing in my life, but all I wanted from Samantha was for her to get out of the car so I could move on to the next ride. I was lonely, but Max had already given me what I needed most.

·  ·  ·

I wasn't the only one that was cash-strapped and desperate. From the beginning, Uber has had an endless appetite for money. Driver rates were slashed again and again over the years, with changes always worded in ways that made it sound like drivers would benefit. Uber always portrayed any change to compensation as a net benefit for drivers. The subtle changes worked, and Uber began to claim that it was moving toward a profitability that was always just out of reach. By prioritizing how much the company was growing, the venture capitalists and investors who were funding the company had their worries soothed. Pay no attention to the cash bonfire happening each year, for the company would one day turn a profit. It would all be worth it once the company went public.

At every point along this expansion, Uber promised its investors that profitability would come at a hazy point in the near future. Once the company finished expanding, it could focus on making money, but once that happened, the message shifted. Profitability would come once the company had perfected self-driving cars or had enough market share, or maybe once it expanded operations to things like food delivery or freight operations. When each of these promises failed to materialize, a new set of promises would appear. Self-driving cars were abandoned as too difficult, and the company quietly sold off the section responsible for them.

Uber expanded all across the globe, but the balance sheets still showed huge losses. The goalposts shifted again and again and again, and along the way, the money burned in a great bonfire. For more than thirteen years, Uber failed to turn a profit but always promised that profits were just around the corner.

The coming of the IPO led to a delicate problem for Uber. The company did not make money, and its leadership knew it. Becoming a public company would mean making internal financial numbers available for scrutiny, and that invited disaster. To obfuscate the obvious failure of a company wholly dependent on being propped up by dwindling cash reserves, Uber needed a metric that it could point to, something that it couldn't get in trouble for claiming but also could be used to bamboozle possible investors.

In the world of finance and accounting, there are certain methods that are used to show the inflow and outflow of cash from a company. These methods are taught to accountants and help to standardize the earnings reports of companies all across the world. Investors rely on the standardized format of these reports to be able to compare the financial strength of one company to another. In the US, companies are required by law to adhere to this format. These accounting principles are generally accepted to give a clear picture of a company's finances, and thus, they are called Generally Accepted Accounting Principles (GAAP).

Among these GAAP measures is a fairly boring number known as EBITDA: earnings before interest, taxes, depreciation, and amortization. You don't need to be an accountant or have any real understanding of finance in relation to that term, but do remember that EBITDA is a real accounting measure used by actual companies for all sorts of things.

How does this relate to Uber? Prior to the IPO, Uber could keep its actual finances a secret, reporting only what it wanted investors to know, but once the company was going to have to list itself publicly, there would be an obligation to share accurate financial metrics. The company's leadership faced an existential question: How could they continue making the company *appear* to be moving toward profitability even if it wasn't? The answer was simple: misdirection.

Uber's financial reports began to feature lots of information about the company's finances, its expansion, and how many rides were being given. Alongside boring earnings numbers were all sorts of facts and figures about the number of active drivers and what percentage of each ride's cost was taken by the company, but all of these extra figures were second in importance to Uber's crown jewel: *adjusted* EBITDA.

Just like the GAAP measure, adjusted EBITDA supposedly measures earnings before interest, taxes, depreciation, and amortization, but it adds back in certain expenses. In Uber's case, the "adjustment" added back in just enough to make the company appear to be making progress. Usually intended to be an internal figure, Uber proudly touted its adjusted EBITDA at every possible opportunity. Its 2021 annual proxy report for investors used the term fifty-four times, often only referring to it as EBITDA and clarifying that it meant the *adjusted* number in footnotes. Buried at the end of the report, in appendix A, is a reconciliation of regular earnings vs. the claimed adjusted EBITDA number. The difference? The actual revenue number reports a loss of nearly $7 billion compared to the adjusted loss of $2.5 billion.[5]

Why does this matter? It matters because EBITDA is a GAAP measure, recognized by accounting principles as a real measure of a tangible thing, and adjusted EBITDA isn't. Uber takes enormous pains to mention at the bottom of its financial disclosures that adjusted EBITDA is a nonstandard measure, and then it immediately refers to this entirely meaningless number over and over again to claim movements toward the goal of profitability.

Even when Uber used this measure, it wouldn't be until the fourth quarter of 2021 that it would finally, finally announce a quarterly profit. In the third quarter, Uber proudly announced it had made an adjusted EBITDA profit of $8 million.[6] This minuscule profit was met with glowing headlines in the press even as the articles themselves often noted that the company still hadn't turned an actual profit.[7] A real profit would have to wait until the second quarter of 2023, when Uber reported a profit of $394 million. A footnote in the press release mentions that the company "earned" $386 million of that profit by revaluing its investments.[8]

Criticism of Uber's financial statements has been fairly muted in the press, with most articles referencing the lack of profits only briefly before returning to repeating the contents of the company's press releases. Among certain financial analysts, however, the criticism is fierce. Transportation analyst Hubert Horan has followed Uber's financial reports from the very beginning, laying out in excruciating detail the three most important points: Uber doesn't make money, Uber has lost tens of billions of dollars while pretending that it can make money, and Uber's claims to the contrary are nonsense.[9] One particularly vehement critic, Cory Doctorow, called Uber an obvious con that had relied on convincing investors that "a pile of shit this big must have a pony under it."[10]

The brazenness of this deception would be laughable if it hadn't worked. The company went public, and all the early investors were able to pass off their holdings to unsuspecting suckers who believed that the company had to be the next big thing. The venture capital funds got their money back in spades, as did the sovereign wealth funds and the few early investors who had financed the company's cash bonfire. As soon as the IPO's "lockup" period ended, founder Travis Kalanick immediately began to liquidate his holdings in the company.[11] Within two months of the first day he could sell his shares, Kalanick resigned from the board of the company and dumped every share he held, walking away with more than $2.5 billion.[12]

In the meantime, the CEO who replaced Kalanick, Dara Khosrowshahi, has done an admirable job of keeping the various plates spinning, but even he cannot keep claiming that the hazy mirage in the distance is an oasis. As the company continues to hemorrhage money and keep itself afloat with various accounting tricks, the end is looming. At some point, the money will run out, and no amount of creative bookkeeping will allow the company to keep operating. Khosrowshahi seems to know that this day is coming. In an email to Uber employees in May 2022, he told staff that a "seismic shift" was occurring. From now on, Uber would focus on "free cash flow" instead of nebulous EBITDA targets.[13] You know, *actual* money.

· · ·

Uber isn't alone in using these sorts of financial tricks to describe itself. Other gig companies are in the same boat. Lyft, Uber's primary competitor in North America, also uses the adjusted EBITDA trickery. It has never reported a profit. It's not just rideshare that has this problem. The food-delivery service DoorDash has never turned a profit either despite using all sorts of tactics to try to juice its income, including a 2020 scandal in which the company was accused of stealing tips from its own drivers.[14]

Uber is only the most prominent example of a greater trend, and rather than looking at gig companies as individual cases, it helps to ask what the movement toward fragmented, piecemeal work is intended to create. After Uber's explosive success, dozens of apps and services began describing themselves as "Uber for X," where X is any product or service that a person could ever want. These companies have been financed with oceans of venture capital, and their effect on society has been corrosive.

There are multiple levels of promises being made, each to different groups, but they are all misleading. To the investors, the app companies claim that they will grow explosively to the point of market domination, at which point they will be able to generate a steady revenue stream by exploiting their monopoly. To the consumer, the promise is an on-demand service, convenience at the tap of a screen. Anything you could ever want can be brought to you at a moment's notice.

For the gig workers, the promise is different but no less misleading. The apps advertise that there is easy money waiting to be made by those who are willing to hustle for it. Fabulous wages, far above the median US income, are available to those willing to put in the hours delivering packages or picking up groceries or driving strangers. No special skills are needed, just determination and plenty of hard work. It's the American Dream, calling from your pocket. Won't you pick up?

This promise is best embodied by an infamous advertisement for the gig service Fiverr, a platform that lets freelancers list their skills and contract for one-off jobs. In a series of ads, the service lauded the "doers" with photos of black-and-white figures who mocked people dreaming of a better life with slogans like "thinking big is still just thinking." The worst of these ads featured a gaunt, exhausted woman staring directly into the camera. "You eat a coffee for lunch. You follow through on your follow through. Sleep deprivation is your drug of choice. You might be a doer," the ad stated without a hint of self-awareness of the horror it was promoting. The message is the embodiment of everything that the gig economy promises to workers. All one has to do to find success and a better life is to get out there and put in the hours, to be willing to do the work. If you don't make it, that's your own fault.

This tangled web of promises exists in tension with itself, for there's no way for the app companies to square their promises to each of their constituencies. The companies don't make money, but they promise desperately that if they can only have a few more years, profitability is just around the corner. The cash reserves burn and burn while the companies grow, and never is the promise kept that the balance sheets will be in the black. The best that investors in these companies have managed is to dump their shares onto more gullible suckers. In Uber's case, the very premise of the company is a lie. People use the app because it is cheaper and more convenient than a traditional taxi, and if the price of a ride is too high, customers won't bite. The only way for the company to make money on each ride would be to charge significantly more, but the moment that an Uber costs as much as a traditional taxi, the edge of the app-based platform fades. The taxi industry is one app away from an identical service, and in many cities, cab companies are already adapting by releasing their own apps with identical ride-hailing features.

For the consumers and drivers, the promises exist as a tug-of-war. An app can be cheap for consumers or profitable for gig workers, but it can't be both. Consumers are promised convenience, but without the drivers, Uber struggles to maintain its on-demand-service promise. Every time that Uber cuts driver pay to juice revenue numbers, the number of active drivers drops. Customers end up with long waits and high prices from surges. The company then spends hundreds of millions of dollars on driver incentives and bonuses to draw drivers back in, but these are cash costs that drive up the price of a ride if they're passed on to the rider. Instead, Uber burns even more money to write them off as a business expense. Drivers come back for the bonuses but won't stick around once they're gone.

Even if you never intend to set foot in the gig economy, its influence is causing a steady decay in traditional working conditions. Because gig companies refuse to classify their workers as employees, they don't have to provide them with benefits or pay into things like unemployment insurance pools, and this has effects that extend far outside the gig economy. One report found that Uber and Lyft would owe California alone $413 million in unemployment funds if their drivers were classified as employees.[15] After California passed a law in 2019 known as AB5 that would have forced gig companies to classify their workers as employees, Uber, Lyft, and DoorDash refused to comply.[16] Instead, the companies (joined by Instacart and Postmates) spent $200 million to finance a successful 2020 ballot initiative known as Proposition 22 that exempted ridesharing and delivery companies from the new labor standards.[17]

Writing gig workers out of labor protections had an immediate effect on more than just the Uber drivers, Instacart pickers, and DoorDash Dashers. Albertsons grocery stores in California took advantage of the law to fire its entire fleet of unionized delivery drivers and replace them with third-party (read: gig) delivery services.[18] For businesses, it only makes sense to fire expensive employees and replace them with unaffiliated contractors who are controlled by an app, especially if they are unionized. From the corporate perspective, unionized workers are expensive trouble-makers who can strike if they aren't treated well. Gig workers are much easier to control: they are fragmented, disorganized, and too desperate to be able to rebel against poor working conditions.

On May 10, 2019, Silicon Valley's darling unicorn premiered on the New York Stock Exchange with dazzling fanfare. Press stories gave breathless coverage to the great disruptor, Uber, the company that had forever changed the way we lived and worked, but for me, May 10 was just another Friday, albeit the day before my birthday.

Amid the endless rides, my phone vibrated with a message from Uber. In celebration of their IPO, the company was going to share its newfound wealth with the people who had built its success. I scoffed at the positive corporate doublespeak but kept reading. Drivers would receive cash bonuses based on the length of their service and how many rides they had completed for the app. The longest-serving drivers would receive $10,000. Others would get $1,000. For the thousands of rides that I had done for the app, my share of the windfall would be $100.

I pulled into a parking lot to read the message again, sure that I had missed some detail. Uber's IPO had been all over the news. Many of the corporate employees who owned stock in the company would become overnight millionaires. The people who would never sit behind the wheel were now wealthy in a way that meant they would never have to work again. They would never have to scrub vomit out of a car's backseat, deal with blacked-out passengers, or be cursed at by an angry drunk for missing a turn. They had done none of the actual work but reaped all the rewards. All of my and other drivers' suffering and sacrifice, the countless rides we had given in order to survive, had made them rich. Our reward was a pat on the back and a payment just small enough to be insulting.

I canceled my next pick up, logged off, and drove home. Kalanick was a billionaire. I was taking the night off.

## CHAPTER 7

MY DAY JOB BECAME A REFUGE AMID ALL THE TURMOIL OF MY LIFE. IN THE office, I could focus my attention on the projects and tasks assigned to me, on reading analysis or profiling the many, many subjects available to us. My attention span had faltered and my assignments took longer to complete because of my frequent hangovers, but I still did a good job on the work I handed in. At least, I thought I did.

It was the beginning of a new school year, with college football season in full swing and the students partying their hearts out when my boss sent me a meeting invite for Friday afternoon labeled "Discussion." Also invited to the meeting was my boss's boss. And her boss. And the chief of intelligence. With so many layers of management in the meeting, there was only one conclusion to be drawn: I was being fired.

I watched the minutes tick by and tried to imagine how I would make ends meet without the salary from my day job. Opening a spreadsheet, I did a quick budget and tried to picture various scenarios that didn't end with being evicted from my apartment. None of them worked. I tried to imagine how I would be able to get by, at least for a while, without a place to live. By the time my laptop dinged to remind me of the meeting's start, I had already worked out a plan for living in my car.

I could keep food in the trunk that wouldn't spoil. A gym membership would allow me to have a place to shower (and maybe find the time to work out that my out-of-shape body needed). The library had computers I could use to look for another job, and Alex and I could pass our days at parks or museums. I would be able to make it work for a few months as long as the nights weren't too cold. With a plan formed in my mind, I closed my laptop and took the short walk to the conference room where I assumed something akin to an execution awaited me.

An hour later, I walked out to my car. Given the news I'd just received, I had permission to take the rest of the day off. Contrary to my expectations, I hadn't been fired, but it was a near thing. I sat down in the driver's seat and let out the longest sigh of my life. The memories washed over me as I tried to figure out whether to go home or turn on the app.

My career as a counterterrorism analyst was over. The increasingly poor job I was doing at work had been papered over as long as possible by the people above me, but it could no longer be tolerated. The work was too sensitive, and there was no room for dead weight in a unit that had to be agile. The chief of intelligence had looked me in the eye and told me that he could fire me, but he had seen what the divorce had done to me. He knew I was an exhausted wreck and had no desire to put me in an even worse position. Instead, I was to be transferred to a different, less sensitive section.

Rather than profiling terrorism suspects, I would be left to look into the coldest of cold cases. All across the state, people who had died without being identified were entered into a database and generally forgotten about. Now, it would be my job to try to come behind every detective, coroner, and medical examiner in the state and try to figure out what they had missed. There was nothing sensitive that could be messed up, no time crunch for answers. It was the career equivalent of being stuffed into a closet to be forgotten.

My coworkers would be told that I had taken a new position voluntarily, a lateral transfer to try something in a different field. My boss left the decision of what to tell the other members of my unit to my discretion. I could tell them the truth or give them the same story that would be told to everyone else in the intelligence section. The choice was mine. In two weeks, I would be moved to missing persons. Until then, my only responsibilities were to finish up my few remaining assignments, meet my new boss, and say goodbye.

I tried to find a silver lining to what had happened, to find some sort of value in my brush with ruin. I found none. Instead, I had gotten lucky that the people who had seen me fall apart decided to take pity on me. My inability to care for myself had finally caught up to me, but I could see no way to fix things. I was so far from a steady and stable life that the best outcome for my slow-moving breakdown was to be grateful to be swept under the rug rather than discarded entirely.

As I turned the key in the ignition, I considered my options. I could go home and toast the death of my dream job by crawling into a bottle, or I could turn on the app and get an early start on Friday night's driving. I decided that I would rather stay in the driver's seat than head back to the sad little hole that I called home. One fast-food cheeseburger later, I was up and running, trying desperately to forget about how close I had come to losing my biggest resource: my job.

■   ■   ■

As a new school year dawned for the college students, so did the first year of preschool for Alex. Marie agreed to meet me in the parking lot on the first day so that we could walk him in together, a moment of cooperative unity for us. From the beginning, Alex struggled at school, often throwing tantrums that led school officials to send him home for the day.

While he was usually on his best behavior when one of us arrived to pick him up, coloring quietly or playing in an empty conference room, the trouble would sometimes start again in the car. When we questioned Alex about what had happened at school, he would tell us impossible stories that drifted between fantasy and reality. When we told him that certain things weren't possible (ninjas had not attacked the school), he would demand that we believe him. His anger would flare as we told him that we wanted the truth so we could know what had actually happened. Alex's tantrums were epic and would last until he had exhausted himself. He would sometimes lock onto a single idea or thought and become fixated so deeply that he would fight us to the point of physical exhaustion, crying in limp rage as he continued attempting to bite us. Marie had told me about a recent incident in which he had kicked the center console of her car so hard that he had broken the hinge on it. Another kick had caved in the small slats of an air-conditioning vent in the backseat.

All of these worries of violence and misbehavior came to a head one Friday. What had been a long and stressful day at work was compounded by a raging headache caused by a particularly late night of heavy drinking. I was suffering through the final hours of the workday when Marie messaged me to ask if I could pick up Alex from his afterschool program. She was trapped on a call that seemed to have no intention of ending and wouldn't be able to get there in time. I squinted my way into the afternoon sunshine and went to pick him up.

When I arrived, I could tell Alex was close to boiling over. Something about the day had gone poorly, and he knew he would be in trouble. As I led him to the car, I tried to reassure him that it was Friday and things would be alright. It was the weekend, and wasn't it nice that Dad had come to pick him up? I buckled him into his car seat and told him we would have our day together on Sunday. As soon as the words left my mouth, I knew I had made a mistake.

"Today isn't a Daddy day?" he asked. No, I explained, it was Friday. Daddy would be out tonight working as the Taxi Man. As I made my way to the driver's side of the car, Alex was already beginning to kick the back of the passenger seat. As we made the short drive from the school to the house, I tried to reassure Alex that we would have our day soon. It's so good to get to see you on a Friday, I told him.

What sounded to me like comforting words enraged Alex, who twisted in his car seat and began trying to reach his feet out to kick me as I drove. Pulling into the neighborhood where Marie lived, I spotted her car in the driveway already. Putting on my best impression of a stern father, I told Alex to calm down and stop kicking. With the car in park beside the house, I turned around to face him, leaning just far enough between the seats for one of his flailing kicks to strike me square between the eyes.

I reeled backward in shock as Alex began thrashing in his car seat, aiming blow after blow against the center console. The same episode that had damaged Marie's car was happening again, but her car wasn't the means of her survival. In a flash, my mind raced with the idea that Alex would damage my car to the point that I wouldn't be able to drive. He would break something, and a rider would complain about the shabby interior of my car. Uber would freeze my driver account, and I would be ruined. Scared, sleep-deprived, and with my head aching for two different reasons, I snapped.

I turned around and lunged at Alex, grabbing his feet and shoving them against his chest.

"Don't you ever hurt this car!" I screamed. He shrank back in the car seat as I leaned toward him and pointed at the house with the yellow door that was supposed to be our family's starter home. Terrified, Alex went wide-eyed and completely still as I ranted at him.

"Do you see that house? Do you see that house filled with all the toys and games and fun things? You have it because of me! You have it because I go out and drive people I don't even know around for hours every night. I work myself to death for you, you ungrateful little bastard, and I will not let you hurt this car. Don't you ever hurt this car!"

I screamed the last sentence in a pure rage filled with every ounce of resentment at the life I had been reduced to, a life of dead dreams and nonexistent hopes where the best I could hope for was scraping together the money not to starve. I closed my eyes and took several deep breaths. Alex was breathing in ragged gasps in his car seat, so panicked by his father's transformation into a screaming madman that he couldn't take a single real breath. When I realized that I was hovering over him, I slumped back into my seat. As I disappeared from in front of him, Alex burst into tears.

I unbuckled my seatbelt and leaned back into the headrest. After a few more deep breaths, I turned around and began trying to apologize to the bawling child in my backseat. I unbuckled his car seat and told him that I was sorry, that Daddy was very tired and should never have yelled at him like that.

"Am I going to lose my bedroom?" Alex asked. It was a child's question, filled with a child's fears, but it burned like poison in my soul. No, I told him, I would never let that happen. You and your mom will never have to leave the house. Daddy promises. I reached toward him to dry his tears with a fast-food napkin from my glovebox and saw the uncertainty as he shrank away from me.

I spent the next few minutes talking quietly with Alex, reiterating that what I had done was wrong and wouldn't happen again. I was very tired, I told him, and I was having a bad day. As a grown-up, I should never have yelled at him. I told him that I loved him with all my heart, that I missed him all the time. I handed him the small stuffed bear that sat in my cupholder and told Alex that he was my little bear, and Daddy carried this so that he would always be with me. With both of our eyes red, we finally got out of the car and walked to the front door of the house.

"Everything alright?" Marie asked as I unlocked the front door.

"Dad yelled at me!" Alex said immediately. "It was scary!" Marie gave me a hard, disapproving look that reminded me of our worst arguments. I told her what had happened. She hugged Alex and told him that it was okay, that I hadn't meant it. Adults do things they don't mean when they're tired, she said. After comforting Alex, she told him that I would be leaving now. I asked Alex if I could have a hug before I left. He hid behind the couch, sticking his head out so I could see him shaking it. Marie motioned toward the door.

"I think you've done enough."

I made it as far as the end of the street before the tears came, racking sobs that choked me so harshly that I had to pull over. With my eyes blurred and nose running, I wailed in shame at the damage I had done in just a few moments. How much of this would Alex remember? What kind of father was I being, to lose my temper and scream at my child for throwing a tantrum solely because he wanted me to be around?

I wept for so long that I lost track of time. My mind relived the incident over and over again. Alex's shaking terror, his gasps and tears, all of it was etched permanently into my mind in an acid-burning shame. When I was finally able to lift my head, I drove to a nearby gas station and washed my face in its dirty sink. My eyes were puffy and red. My nose was so clogged that I was forced to breathe through my mouth. I resisted the urge to punch the idiot in the mirror before walking out to my car, buckling in, and logging on to drive for the night. I squinted my way through the sunset as I drove toward FSU and told myself that it would be night soon. No one would be able to see my reddened eyes in the dark.

After spending a few hours with the college students, I accepted a suburb ride as a chance to have a quiet moment away from the crowds. As I wound my way through the dark streets of the upper-middle-class neighborhood, I marveled at the manicured lawns and giant houses. They were a short drive but a world apart from my apartment, with shiny new cars in the driveways and not a railroad track in sight. As I sat in the driveway awaiting my passenger, I was overwhelmed with bitterness at the fact that I would never be able to have something like this. For all my hard work, the best I could manage was scraping by and narrowly avoiding being fired.

When the car door finally opened, I was surprised at the skinny young man who hopped in the backseat. Dressed in cutoff jean shorts and a white T-shirt, Tyler's hair was dyed platinum blond and slicked back, making him look like a third-rate Eminem impersonator. He thanked me for coming out to get him before making a comment that piqued my curiosity.

"It's really hard to get an Uber out here sometimes, and I really need to go out tonight. I'm not allowed to drive right now, so if you hadn't picked me up, I don't know what I would have done." I took a moment to mull over what he might have meant, ultimately deciding that Tyler likely had a suspended license. Judging by his fashion sense, I was betting on a DUI. With miles to go before we reached the college bar that Tyler had entered as his destination, I nudged him to say more by asking how he'd lost his license.

"Well, I didn't lose it," he said slowly. I could tell he was debating how much he wanted to reveal. "The judge took it away."

"What for?" I asked. Tyler shifted uncomfortably in the passenger seat and pulled on his seatbelt. He turned to look out the window at the houses rolling past.

"I got arrested by the DEA for cocaine trafficking."

I paused for a few extra moments at a stop sign. Cocaine trafficking? The kid sitting next to me had gotten arrested for trying to be Pablo Escobar? I thought about my work badge, stuffed in the center console, and wondered how much of the story Tyler would be willing to tell me. I prodded with a few questions but mostly let Tyler talk. I'd learned that the best way to get someone to open up was to fill the air with uncomfortable silence.

Tyler told me that he'd started selling weed in high school for extra money, and when he went to college in Tampa, he'd made a connection that let him branch out into selling cocaine. Flush with money from selling to his fellow college students, he'd dropped out of school without telling his parents. A regular customer had introduced him to a friend that purchased small amounts off of him. After a few months, the friend said he was throwing a party and wanted to make a bigger purchase than usual.

"I should have known something was up," Tyler said, "but it was a ton of money. I pulled in to his apartment, and then this van pulled in behind me. That's when guys with guns jumped out and started screaming at me to get on the ground." To no one's surprise except Tyler's, his new customer had turned out to be a federal agent. One of his regular customers had been arrested and turned on him by introducing him to the undercover. Tyler, in turn, rolled over on everyone he knew to try to get a more lenient sentence. He'd been allowed to live with his parents while awaiting sentencing. I tried to find a way to tell Tyler that I was sorry that he was going to go to prison, but he cut me off.

"I mean . . . I did it to myself," he said. "It's my fault." He sighed as we reached the strip of college bars near his destination. "This is probably my last chance to go out for a while. I need to get laid before I go away, you know?" I put aside my doubts that he and his jean shorts would be able to entice the college girls into sleeping with him and said that I understood. As we pulled into the parking lot of his destination, Tyler unbuckled his seatbelt and stared at the line of people waiting to get in. After a few moments, he sighed again.

"You know what I feel worst about? It's not that I'm gonna go to jail. I let my parents down. They had to sell the house to pay for the lawyer. I grew up in that house, and now it's gonna be gone because I fucked up. It sucks." He reached for the door handle. "Anyway, you don't give a shit about all that. Thanks for the ride." I watched Tyler walk away and thought about Alex. Even in the dreamy, McMansion-filled suburbs, it only took a few mistakes for your actions to ripple outward and upend the lives of people around you.

■   ■   ■

Meanwhile, Alex's behavioral issues continued to cause problems at school. Marie or I would be summoned to pick him up at least two to three days per week for fighting, biting, or having some sort of tantrum from which he couldn't calm down.

Working the crowd of a late Saturday football game, I tried to stay cheerful and put my problems out of my mind. Filled with caffeine, I laughed and joked with the passengers that were sober enough to hold a conversation. I endured the obnoxious frat boys and entitled alumni as I racked up fare after fare in the surge zones, expertly navigating the crowded streets and police road-blocks that were a gameday tradition at FSU. The police seemed to block roads around the stadium at random, opening and closing streets with no discernible rhyme or reason, and learning to track which routes were available was a game of cat and mouse that I enjoyed winning.

As the game neared its end, I was called to a bar in the middle of downtown. As I navigated the choked streets, my phone buzzed with a text message. At a red light, I stopped to read it:

Marie: *Alex is out of control. Can you call me?*

My heart raced as I wondered what to do. It wasn't my day with Alex, but if he was having trouble, I didn't want to turn away from that. I debated ignoring the message and continuing to work. Still several minutes from the pickup point, I tapped to call back. My desire to help my son outweighed my selfish emotions. Marie picked up immediately.

"I'm sorry to call you," she said. "I wouldn't do it if I thought I could handle it, but I don't know what to do. Alex has been hitting and kicking me for two hours. I can't get him to calm down, and I can't keep getting beaten up." I could hear my son yelling and throwing things at his mother as she pleaded with him to stop. I nosed my car through another intersection, dodging the relentless crowds of revelers and looking for a parking spot near my pickup point. I told myself that my rider probably wouldn't show up for a few minutes and began trying to talk to Alex.

I told him all the things we'd discussed before, that it was okay to have big feelings, but that was when we needed to ask for help. I told him that it was never okay to hit people because we were upset, that everyone deserved to feel safe. Marie interrupted me to say that she had already told him all of this, and none of it had helped. As another round of scuffling and yelling came through the speakers, my car door opened. I quickly punched the mute button on my phone as a trio of slurring twentysomethings climbed into my backseat. Panicking, I quickly explained that I was a divorced father and my son was having a total meltdown with his mother. I told them that I could still give them the ride, but I could only do it if they agreed to be totally silent and let me try to talk to my son. They buckled in and nodded their agreement. I swiped to start the ride, put the car in drive, and unmuted the phone.

I tried to pick up where I had left off, telling Alex that I understood that he felt overwhelmed by his feelings, but his mother wasn't the enemy. She was trying to help him, and the best thing he could do was trust her and let her help. Pushing through the sudden traffic of the football game's end, I glanced in the mirror at my passengers, mercifully quiet and looking at their phones. I kept going with my fatherly pep talk, but nothing helped. Alex's mind was on fire, and every word from me or Marie only added fuel to the inferno. As the minutes stretched on, the men in the backseat began to talk quietly, showing each other things on their phones.

"What is that?" Marie suddenly asked. "Do you have people in your fucking car with you?"

"I'm working right now," I said. "You texted me while I was on the way to pick someone up and . . ."

"I don't give a shit," she said. "Why don't you call me back when you can make your son a priority." The line went dead.

"Damn dude, she's pissed," mumbled the man in the middle of the backseat before going back to scrolling through his Instagram feed.

The other two men began apologizing, but I could hardly hear their words. My body broke into a cold, stress-induced sweat, and my only desire was to get these three idiots out of my car. It had been a simple request, to sit quietly, and they couldn't even do that. I debated pulling over and ordering them out of my car before remembering the massive surge attached to the ride. This was worth too much money to give up.

I resolved instead to get them back to their apartment complex as fast as I could. As we rolled to a stop at a red light, I noticed that the traffic ahead of me was being redirected by a police officer. With rising alarm, I realized that with the football game ending, the police had reversed the flow of traffic in the one-way streets around the stadium. Routes that normally would have been open were now choked with double lanes of fans heading home. To get the men back to their apartment, I would need to find a way past the traffic.

I darted down a side street and was pushed into the flow of outward traffic by a cop with a light-up wand. A few streets later, I tried again with the same result. With hundreds of cars between me and my destination, the only thing on my mind was Alex. What was he doing while his dad was panicking in a car on the other side of town? Was he crying? Hitting his mother? Why didn't I cancel this stupid ride and put him first?

Nearly half an hour later, the obnoxious trio in the backseat finally got out. What should have taken ten minutes had required a diversion far south of the stadium, multiple side streets, and far too much waiting in traffic. My shirt was soaked in cold sweat. My back ached from tensing, and my hands were white from gripping the wheel until my knuckles hurt. I pulled into a parking spot in an empty lot and tapped to call Marie back.

She answered immediately. In the background, I could hear the quiet sobs of Alex, exhausted and emotionally spent from his meltdown. Marie told me that they were in his bedroom, wrapped up in a blanket and hugging each other as they talked. I started asking questions delicately, trying to probe Alex for answers. I quietly asked him what had happened, but his answers were as incoherent as ever. Alex could never explain his moods or what caused them, and asking him about them often seemed to confuse him. Please, I pleaded, try to remember. What was the problem that started all this?

"I think we both know what the problem is," Marie interjected. "The problem is you aren't here. He doesn't want me; he wants both of us. He wants the house and the family that we promised him. You show up every other day and we play family, but you're not really here. You're not even doing the hard parts. Most of the time, you're gone, and even when you're here, you aren't really present. You're just going through the motions, and we're both sick of it."

The words stung me into silence. I tried several times to say something, but words escaped me. I thought back on every game of hide-and-seek that I'd pushed through despite a hangover, every episode of cartoons I'd snoozed through on the couch. I was physically present, but she was right. Often, I was too exhausted to really engage. She was doing the hard parts of raising our son. I was too busy surviving to be what he needed.

Burning with shame, I asked Alex if he got angry with his mother because she wasn't me. There was no reply from Alex, but Marie told me he was nodding his head.

"We need to work something out where he can spend time with both of us, but not together. It's too confusing for him for you to come and go, and frankly, I'm tired of having you around. I know you say your place isn't set up, but you need to get it together. We can't keep doing this to him. All it's doing is confusing him."

Tears in my eyes, I told her that I would figure something out.

"I think he's calm now," she said to me, then to him "Let's try to get to bed." I could hear Alex mutter his assent. "We'll see you tomorrow." I choked out a goodnight to Alex as the call ended. Underneath the buzzing of a streetlight, I let the emotions consume me. I beat the steering wheel in frustration. A broken marriage, a broken life, and now, a broken child.

# CHAPTER 8

THAT NIGHT WAS THE POINT WHERE I COULD NO LONGER STAND TO HIDE MY emotions in a haze of liquor. As the next week started, I called every psychiatrist's office in town and asked for an appointment. Some offices told me that they weren't accepting patients or had a wait of several months for an appointment. Finally, I found one that could see me the next week. As I filled out the intake paperwork and dropped it off after work, I couldn't help but feel lucky. I logged on to start my driving for the night and thought about the resources I had that weren't available to other drivers.

There weren't many benefits of working for the State of Florida. The pay was low, raises were unheard of, and the opportunities for advancement were minimal, but one thing I did have was health insurance. The insurance wasn't accepted by every doctor, but by paying just $50 per month, I somehow had excellent coverage. The drivers who were working full-time behind the wheel had nothing. Classified as independent contractors, we were owed (and given) nothing by Uber. Although the app would helpfully point drivers toward health insurance exchanges, there was no financial assistance available. For all the damage that sitting for hours on end was doing to my body, the app took no responsibility.

While I had originally tried to take decent care of myself while I was driving, the urge to take stretching and bathroom breaks later gave way to the fear of missing a ride. On busy nights, logging off to get out and stretch might mean missing out on a surge, and pulling over to take a bathroom break could mean losing a bonus for taking multiple rides in a row. Especially on Friday nights, I would stay behind the wheel for four to five hours at a time, driving even as both my back and bladder ached. The lack of available bathrooms after midnight meant that I had pissed in quite a few dark parking lots around town, sometimes waving goodbye to one passenger before driving down the road to find convenient bushes where I could relieve myself. Even when I took these "breaks," I brought my phone with me so that I wouldn't miss a ping.

As my first psychiatrist appointment loomed, I began seeking someone to assess my physical health. The past few years had left my body an absolute wreck. During the worst moments before the end of my marriage, I'd stopped eating from the stress, shedding nearly thirty pounds. Now, I'd managed to put all of that weight back on in the form of a softness made up of liquor, salt, and fried foods. I found a doctor who was accepting patients and scheduled a physical for the same week as my psychiatric assessment.

What followed was a series of appointments that probably saved my life. At the psychiatrist's office, I had barely finished describing my personal habits before the psychiatrist told me I had a textbook case of obsessive-compulsive disorder. Disturbed, I insisted that wasn't possible. I didn't wash my hands or fix my door locks a thousand times a day, and the only reason my apartment was so clean was because I was never there. I didn't need to check on things endlessly.

"What worries you?" he asked.

Everything, I told him. My whole life was worry. There were so many things that could go wrong, and I had to keep track of them all so that I wouldn't get surprised. Look at how I was living. Who wouldn't worry?

"When someone upsets you, do you let it go easily?"

Definitely not, I said. I tended to think about rude people in my backseat for days at a time, imagining a thousand different ways that I could have handled the situation better.

"That's called ruminating," his nurse cut in. "You start thinking about something and can't stop." It certainly sounded familiar.

"Don't you see, Jon?" he said gently. "The worrying *is* the compulsion." He wrote me a prescription for a high dose of anti-anxiety medication and urged me to look up cognitive behavioral therapy on the internet. There are plenty of free resources, the nurse told me. She would email some to me.

My appointment for a physical went even more poorly. After taking my blood pressure and ordering some lab tests, the doctor gently told me to take better care of myself while writing a prescription for blood pressure medication. A few days later, the bloodwork he had ordered triggered another phone call to place me on cholesterol medication. The nurse that called me put it bluntly: "You're not in imminent danger of a heart attack, but you're certainly working toward one."

The medications from the doctor were cheap generics, drugs that had been on the market for years, but the psychiatric medication was more expensive. The drug was new, and even with my insurance and a voucher from the psychiatrist's office to get it at a steep discount, it was yet another bill that would cause a struggle. I resolved to be more diligent with my plasma donations so I could pay for it.

A few weeks later came a follow-up appointment with the psychiatrist's office. The nurse practitioner who would be monitoring my adjustment to the medication had decorated her office with abstract art and plenty of small objects to fidget with. She smiled and gently asked me how I was adjusting to the medication. I told her that I was less focused but more stable. My ability to hyperfocus on a problem in order to solve it was gone, but so too was my ability to ruminate endlessly on the things that troubled me. For the first time in a long time, I was able to push away things that upset me, to think about them just one time and be done with them.

"Good," she said, tapping notes into her computer. "That's exactly what it's supposed to do."

She told me that I would have to relearn how to focus on important tasks, that I would no longer be able to obsess about a problem until I could solve it. In the long run, this new focus would make me a better, more balanced person. Turning back from her keyboard, she fiddled with a pen as she struggled to find a way to phrase the question she wanted to ask me. After a bit, she found the right words.

"You mentioned that you tended to drink quite a bit . . ." she began. I nodded. "Could you explain what you meant by that?"

I hesitated, not wanting to admit that I was drinking myself to sleep every night, but I eventually opted for the truth. I was here because I wanted help, and it was her job to help me. Lying wouldn't do either of us any good. After describing the generous method I used to pour my ginger ales, she stopped me.

"Have you ever considered stopping that?" she asked. I protested that I had two handles of bourbon and several dozen beers in my fridge. What was I supposed to do with it? She tapped her pen on her crossed knee.

"So? Pour it out. Get rid of it," she deadpanned. "It's not helping you get over your issues. It's just numbing you from finishing the grieving process." She made a few more arguments for halting my excessive drinking. It would help me sleep better, save money, and be a better, more present father for Alex. Her last argument sank into my chest like a weight, and I promised her that I would get rid of the alcohol. She asked if I thought I could stay dry until our next appointment, a month away. I said I would try.

Leaving the office, I detoured to my apartment rather than go to work. I pulled the heavy bottles of liquor out of my freezer and set the beer on my counter. I unscrewed the cap of the opened bottle of bourbon and stared at my sink, wondering if I could really find the strength to pour it down the drain. After a few minutes, I put the cap back on, shoved the bottles in a reusable grocery bag, and carried them with the beer out to my car.

I couldn't bring myself to pour the bottles down the drain or toss them in the dumpster. The time I would spend cracking open fancy IPAs to pour them down my sink could be spent in a better way that might actually make someone else happy. For as much as I hated the college students, I owed them my life, and if these bottles and cans were filled with self-loathing in my hands, perhaps they would be better disposed of by putting them to use.

The lobby of the Kappa Alpha fraternity house was empty when I arrived. The concrete floor was sticky and painted black to hide dirt. The entire house smelled of stale beer and bleach. I'd come in through the back entrance, through a door flanked by a pair of couches that had been left outside in the Florida weather long enough that they likely qualified as biohazards. Inside, a set of cheaply constructed wooden tables showed the lingering evidence of a game of beer pong. They were the only furniture. I called out a hello but heard nothing but the echo of my own voice. Satisfied that I was alone, I went back to my car and retrieved the alcohol. The beer went into a filthy fridge just off the beer pong room. The handles of bourbon were left on the kitchen counter.

Spotting an errant sheet of paper, I grabbed it and quickly jotted down a note thanking the brothers for being unfailingly polite, the only fraternity brothers that I didn't mind driving. I explained that I had decided to quit drinking, and I thought they could put my alcohol to better use. I signed the note "Jon the Uber driver" and left through the back door. I later learned during a ride that the brothers had framed my note and hung it upstairs with a picture of the booze I left them. It wasn't the most responsible way to work toward being a better person, but it was a start.

.  .  .

Besides the health benefits, quitting drinking had one major impact I hadn't anticipated: money. What had started as an occasional trip to the liquor store had bloomed into a constant habit, and once I stopped, I found myself with cash I hadn't realized I had. It left me with choices to make. There was an endless list of things that I needed in my apartment, and little by little, I started to acquire them. I had done without so many things for so long that when I finally had the chance to acquire them, I didn't know where to begin. I started with small purchases, things that would give me a little more comfort without feeling like I was spending too much money. Some towels for the bathroom that weren't quite as threadbare. New socks. A coffee maker so that I didn't have to drink the instant stuff anymore. There were bigger things I needed, but making a large purchase felt risky. I remained as afraid as ever that this entire enterprise might suddenly collapse, and my fear kept me from thinking about anything but the most immediate concerns.

This is part and parcel of the logic of poverty. Because you are forced to constantly reckon with small decisions, they become comfortable. Anything involving a significant amount of money lives only in your fears, not your dreams. Spending $1,000 on a piece of quality furniture feels like an insane decision when you are one missed paycheck away from homelessness. You tell yourself that it makes more sense to buy the cheap IKEA table even though it will fall apart in a few years, and in the realm of the poor, it does. It is far better to have ten cheap things than two expensive ones, and you'll replace them a dozen times before you even consider looking at high-quality stuff that doesn't fall apart.

This behavior leaves you shellshocked in a way that people who live comfortably never have to experience. Because everything you own is cheap, your possessions are always in poor condition. The bookshelf sags in the middle and the veneer of your pressboard TV stand is peeling. Your clothes are faded and your shoes are worn out, but fixing any one of them with a quality product would take more than you are willing to risk. What if the electric bill is higher than you anticipated because of the summer heat? It does no good to have comfortable shoes but be behind on your rent, but in a sick inversion of your needs, constantly replacing your cheap junk when it breaks eats up the money that could be spent on getting something permanent.

You cringe and put up with the constant decay of everything you own because you are too scared to make major investments. Perhaps you can find the willpower to buy yourself a few nice things, but anything more than that is dangerous and likely beyond your means. The harsh deprivation of my existence had taught me why people on food stamps sometimes bought things they didn't need, why kids in the poorest neighborhoods dreamed of nice shoes and sleek cell phones. Sometimes, having just one nice thing was all it took to make you feel like a human being, so you scraped and saved and sacrificed all to have *just one thing* and feel alive again. Even if that one thing isn't a necessity, just the sight of it is an escape from the ever-present fear of financial oblivion.

In my case, there was one purchase that I could put off no longer. I had put up with a tremendous number of indignities in my little apartment: the rumbling trains, dirty hallways, and dingy interiors could be tolerated because I had chosen them. Sleeping on the floor; however, was a daily reminder of how little I had.

With a sick sense of leaping off of a cliff, I hesitantly tapped on my phone to confirm an order for a simple metal frame for my mattress. Though it was hardly a real bed, I paid an extra $40 for it to have a headboard rather than simply being a platform. At $260, it was the most expensive thing I had purchased in a year. As the finished order appeared on the screen, I was overcome with a mix of emotions. Fear and pride swirled in equal measures, while anxiety twisted my stomach into knots as I worried that I had just spent myself into a corner. My phone vibrated as the confirmation landed in my email, promising delivery by next Saturday. I ran to the bathroom to vomit. As I heaved my worries into the toilet, I told myself that I would drive extra hours, just in case.

For the following week, I pushed myself to get behind the wheel every night. On days with Alex, I worked late after he was asleep, not getting home until 11 p.m. On my days to myself, I left after work and stayed out until midnight, fueling myself with dollar-menu fast food and massive amounts of caffeine. I checked and rechecked my bank account and my budget, alternating between reassuring myself that I deserved a real place to sleep and berating myself for indulging in such a stupid luxury. By the time Friday arrived, I was ready to work until the bars closed to make up for my vain and reckless purchase. As I arrived back at my apartment to shower for the night, I found my door blocked by a massive box. The bedframe had arrived a day early.

I quickly dragged it inside and tore it open. My plans for driving that night would have to be put on hold. I didn't care how long it took to assemble, I was sleeping in a bed tonight—a *real* bed. As I laid the disconnected rails on the floor and began screwing them together with the tiny included wrench, I dreamed of the moment when my head would hit the pillow, of the morning when I would wake up and sit in bed with a book and a cup of coffee. Nearly an hour and a half later, I finished tucking the corners of the sheets under the bed. Even the most demanding military drill instructor couldn't have found a single fault. I laid down on top of the bed and stared at the ceiling, now closer to me than I had been accustomed to. Every fiber of my being screamed that I deserved to close my eyes, to revel in just a few moments of this victory. I took a few deep breaths before getting up and heading to my car. It was time to get back to work.

. . .

My time with Alex felt increasingly precious. With my apartment slowly becoming a real home, our days together were now spent building puzzles and playing in the grassy area outside. Alex reacted well to our one-on-one time and my full attention. The behavioral issues that seemed intractable a few months ago were softening, and Marie and I hoped that the progress would continue.

I took an exhausted pride in keeping my promises. Every hour I worked meant earning money that let my son grow up in the home we had wanted for him. Bit by bit, ride by ride, I earned the money that let Alex have a house, a yard, and a place that was safe. I had entered the divorce determined to make him a priority, even at my own expense, and I was succeeding. Every good day at school was a little victory, and every victory gave me the strength to push through my exhaustion. I could work on myself and get better. I could work hard for him, and things would get better. I could help myself, and in doing so, I could help others.

My decision to be a helper began to again extend to my passengers. If a rider needed help loading and unloading groceries, I would jump to lift the bags. I climbed stairs and loaded wheelchairs and walked blind passengers to the curb. I dispensed sage advice to the college students and tried to help them with their problems. If I could help one person find the confidence to break up with an abusive partner, maybe I could be the parent I had always wanted to be. If I could make the world just a little bit better, surely it would rebound on me at some point. I wasn't sure if I believed in karma, but there was no penalty for trying to do good things for people.

Every time I logged on to the app, I told myself I was being given a chance to help someone. The money I made on each ride was slowly shoring up my lifestyle, and while progress was slow, there *was* progress. Driving had allowed me an outlet to explore my own traumas and insecurities, and I had learned how to listen and comfort the pains of others. That I was also being paid during this time was a different issue. Driving had come to serve multiple purposes. It allowed me to survive, fulfill my promises to my son, and feel like a person of value. I had started my driving career as an empty shell, but somehow I had evolved into someone who found purpose in being useful to others.

The most striking example of my newfound determination was meeting a woman named Maria. A college student, Maria called a ride in the middle of Friday night's biggest surge, but she wasn't going out. Already a few drinks in, she'd had enough of pushy fraternity brothers and catty friends. Maria was young and pretty and very, very tired. By this time of night, all Maria really wanted was to go to bed, but before she could do that, she had to wait for her landlord.

Maria had lost her keys at some point during the night, and now she had to wait for someone from the maintenance department of her student apartment to unlock her door and give her a new key. As we pulled in to her complex, I was surprised to see that the apartments seemed evenly split between newly renovated units and a construction zone. On one side were outside stairwells painted a bright yellow and illuminated by dim exterior lights. On the other, wooden staircases creaked in the dark. Small groups of men huddled on the dark exterior walkways of the half-finished building, idly puffing cigarettes in the night. The cigarettes were my first clue that something was amiss. Students didn't smoke— they vaped. Maria sighed beside me.

"I hate this place," she mumbled as she reached for the door. With my suspicions aroused, I asked if she was going to be okay. She let go of the door handle and sat back into the seat.

"You see those guys up there?" she asked, pointing to the men on the walkways. "They're the construction workers renovating the other building. They get to stay in the rooms while they're working on the building, and they're always outside smoking at night. They talk about me whenever they see me. They speak Spanish, but I'm from Miami, so I understand them. It's really gross."

I thought about the situation in which I was about to leave Maria. An intoxicated college student, by herself and locked out of her apartment, about to go stand in the dim light of a near-empty apartment complex while groups of nearby men cat-called about her body? It felt like the opening paragraph to a news story with a tragic ending. I couldn't do it.

With a few quick taps, I told the app to log me off. Even in the middle of the busiest part of the night, it was more important for me to make sure that I wasn't leaving Maria in a bad situation than it was to make a few extra dollars. As much as I needed the money, I needed more to be able to look myself in the mirror and feel like a person that was worth a damn. I told Maria that we could sit here and wait for her landlord together. The relief that filled her face was immediate.

Over the next half hour, I talked to Maria about her classes, the Cuban food she missed from her home, and the friends she'd made at the university. Any topic was fine if it distracted her from the men on the catwalks above us. By the time her phone rang with a call from maintenance, the late-night surge was gone, replaced with the dead zone around midnight when all the students were already where they wanted to be. Maria told me goodnight and hopped out to be let in to her apartment.

A few more hours of rides later, I arrived back at my apartment and fell into bed, into the exhausted, dead sleep of workers whose hopes are subsumed by their struggle to survive. When I woke up the next morning, I rushed through my morning routine and walked back out to my car, ready to pick up the Saturday morning passengers who woke up in stranger's beds. An unusual subset of passengers, they were usually quiet, simple rides because of their hangovers. It was easy money.

As I climbed into the driver's seat, I noticed that my glovebox was open. With a plastic to-go cup of coffee still stinging my hand rather than perking up my mind, it took a few moments to realize that someone had been in my car overnight. The entire scenario confused me. I didn't keep anything valuable in the car because I didn't have anything valuable. There was nothing worth taking in the first place, so why break in?

I did a quick inventory of the things that were missing. The few coins that had been in my cupholders were gone, as was the charging cable for my phone (the car charger had been left behind). A small logbook that I kept in the center console was gone, and with it, the record of all the miles I had driven each night. I was tracking the miles for tax purposes, but now I'd have to guess how far I'd driven in the service of my digital masters. As I took stock of the burgled items, I finally realized that there was one major item missing: the ring.

My wedding band had never been anything fancy. It was a simple golden band, meant to be a symbol of devotion more than a piece of jewelry. With my marriage over, it shouldn't have had any meaning at all, and I had occasionally wondered if I should sell it. A pawnshop where I had stopped during an afternoon break from driving a few months prior had offered me $20 for it, describing it as a "straight melter," a ring to be sold for scrap. I still hadn't been able to give it up. Even if I was only wearing the ring on the nights when I was emotionally vulnerable, it was valuable as a talisman of protection from the truth of my circumstances.

Lately though, I had worn it less and less. Putting on the ring felt like clinging to the past, to a vain hope that my life would somehow undo its ruination. The more I accepted the reality of work, driving, and parenting, the less I needed to be reminded of what could have been. I had a life in front of me, and while it was busy and exhausting, it was my own. I had learned that people could accept me for who I was, and I didn't need to pretend to be anyone else. There was only one person who really mattered, and all he wanted was to play superheroes and spend time with Dad.

The ring was gone, but I had grown beyond it. I didn't need it to protect me anymore. Somehow, in the thousands of people who had passed through my backseat, I had found a way to move on and accept not just my situation but myself. I hadn't been a good husband, but in the aftermath of my own failure, I learned that there were many things that I could be: a good father, a survivor, and a helper to those who needed it.

I didn't need to put on a scratched-up old ring and pretend to be someone I wasn't. When riders asked me why I was in Tallahassee or why I started driving, I told the truth. I had spent years drinking myself into a stupor because I hated myself, hated the failure of a man that looked back at me in the mirror. Now, I stared right back and told him to be better. I had lied endlessly to strangers who would never see me again because I feared their judgment, but no one could ever have punished me more harshly than I had punished myself. I finally saw value in myself, in the man who carried groceries for strangers and loved his son more than anything in the world. I would put good things into the world, and if it didn't want to love me back, that was fine. I'd still try. I'd always try.

I started the car and headed for a nearby gas station to buy a soda and a charging cable for my phone before I logged on. *Look on the bright side*, I told myself. *At least the thieves hadn't broken the window.*

# CHAPTER

9

THE SMALL PART OF ME THAT STILL BELIEVED IN A BETTER FUTURE KNEW THAT I
needed to find a way to survive in case of an emergency. I had
come close to ruin before figuring out that there was extra money
in my veins, but I couldn't risk that again. The students were my
best opportunity to build an emergency fund, and even though
every part of me ached to back off my punishing schedule, I per-
sisted. As the students partied their way through another semes-
ter, I was right there with them. Within a few months, I had saved
an extra $500 from driving and plasma donations. I pulled the
money out of my bank account, wrapped it in a rubber band, and
put it in a mason jar in my sock drawer. It was, quite literally, a
glass to be broken in case of an emergency.

With the emergency fund in place, I took the opportunity to
slow down the schedule that had left me so battered. My physical
health had suffered badly from me pushing myself. Lack of sleep,
combined with my long working hours, contributed to a hazy fog
in my mind that seemed impossible to dissipate. I learned from
experience that plasma donation had lingering effects, especially
when you're bleeding yourself two times a week. A full day after
my visits to the center, I would find myself slumped deeply into

the driver's seat, struggling to stay awake and push away the feeling of being physically drained.

I stopped donating plasma and began cutting back my driving hours. My seventy-hour weeks became more manageable at fifty-five to sixty hours. I slept in on the weekends and took Mondays off from driving. Unsure of what to do with myself, I took up a variety of hobbies, from painting miniature figurines to baking. Around the office, I became known for walking cubicle to cubicle, passing out the latest batch of baked goods so that I wouldn't eat them all myself. The creativity, not the cookies, was the real balm to my soul. I wasn't at the mercy of anyone else's whims. I could create what I wanted, when I wanted, in the way that I wanted. It was real freedom, not the false promises of the apps.

One of the best things that the college kids brought wasn't measured in dollars. Summer riders were an interesting cross section of humanity, but for pure entertainment, nothing surpassed the antics of the students. Where the slow pace of rides during the summer only occasionally left me with an interesting interaction, the students called rides constantly, and the continuous flow of new people in the backseat meant that I experienced the full, vibrant rainbow of their bad behaviors. As much as I told myself they annoyed me, I loved the rapid-fire flow of fresh faces that passed through my backseat.

Of course, students weren't the only people capable of behaving badly. I had learned that in putrid detail from a half-naked, vomit-covered housewife, but something about the university created a gravitational pull that drew in the people most inclined to alcoholic extravagance. Football games had drunken tailgaters and parents' weekend attracted mothers and fathers who tried to keep up the same pace as their children, but homecoming was the weekend with the worst drunks. Former students who had partied hard in their younger years returned to Tallahassee and tried to relive the glory of their youth despite the passage of time. They had no sense of their own limits, or if they did, they certainly didn't show it to me.

Larry and Marnie definitely didn't know their limits anymore. The pair of hefty, middle-aged men shuffled toward my car on a chilly October night with the careful gait that I had come to recognize as a sign of overindulgence. Larry climbed in behind me while Marnie sat on the passenger side of the backseat. I greeted them both. Larry gave me a quick hello while Marnie grunted his response, dropped his head onto chest, and promptly passed out. Larry's response was quick and violent.

"No! No no no no no, you fat fuck! Don't you dare fall asleep! I'm not carrying your 275-pound Samoan ass into the house!"

He punctuated his yelling by slapping Marnie hard across the face, hard enough that his head whipped to the side. Otherwise, Marnie didn't stir. Larry slapped him again, the flat sound echoing in the parking lot. Unsure how to handle the situation, I decided to start by asking if I should call for some help for Marnie.

"Nah man, we don't need no ambulance or nothing; he's just sleepy. Big guys like us, we don't really get sick. We just get sleepy, and I don't want to carry his ass into the house."

He paused to slap Marnie again before sighing in defeat and settling back into his seat.

"I give up. He's out," Larry said, clicking his seatbelt. "Can we swing through Whataburger? I'm buying."

I took a moment to consider my options. The responsible thing to do would be to call for help for Marnie, but that would take up a lot of time when I could be working. In all likelihood,

Marnie was fine, and the bigger risk was that he would wake up suddenly and throw up in my backseat. Then again, if he did, I'd get a hefty payday from the cleaning fee. I decided to risk it, on one condition. I told Larry I'd need a large fry and a refill on my soda. He agreed, and off we went.

Larry told me that he'd met Marnie freshman year, and they'd become fast friends because they were both overweight. They'd lived together off campus, partied together, and supported each other when they decided to start losing weight. They'd returned to Tallahassee to visit some of their favorite bars and see what had changed in the city in the decades since they'd been students.

"He's down to 275, but we're both still working on it," Larry told me. When our food came out of the window at Whataburger, Larry again tried to rouse his friend, first by waving a fry under his nose and then by slapping him a few more times. The only response was gentle snoring.

We made our way to the house that they had rented for the weekend, but it was only when we arrived that I realized we had another problem: how to get Marnie out of the car. The driveway was filled with cars, raising very real questions about how Marnie was going to make his way from the curb to the house.

"You ready to do this?" Larry asked. His voice spoke of the expectation of my assistance, something I had only realized would be necessary when I pulled up at the curb. I got out and walked around to Marnie's side as Larry unbuckled himself. As I opened the door, I leaned around Marnie's slumbering form to ask how Larry wanted to do this.

"Here we go. One, two, three!" he said quickly, shoving Marnie out of the door to land on top of me. I fell back into the grass, smothered in sweaty Samoan manhood. As I struggled to push

Marnie off of me, one of my shoes came off. Larry trotted onto the grass and pulled Marnie to a sitting position before handing me my lost footwear. I put my shoe on. Marnie snored.

We each took one shoulder and half lifted, half dragged the 275 pounds of Marnie's dead weight toward the house. Larry unlocked the door, and we struggled inside to deposit the slumbering Marnie on a green couch upholstered in a flower pattern.

"Thanks, brother, I couldn't have done that without you," Larry said. "I'll make sure to leave you a fat tip on the app."

I told Larry to have a good night and headed back to my car. I ended the ride, taking a moment to appreciate that it was Marnie's name on the account. Larry had no ability to tip me. My favorite lie had made yet another appearance. I stared down at the lukewarm fries that were my reward for going above and beyond. I told myself that I'd done the pair a good deed, that I'd done the right thing, but it was all self-soothing.

From the moment I pulled up outside the bar, it was obvious that I was going to have to carry Marnie into the house. I couldn't have refused the ride; I needed the money. Just like the idea that I could be my own boss, what I had wasn't a real choice but the illusion of a choice. This is what the apps relied on, that they could lay down guidelines and rules, but drivers would never really follow them. The app could tell drivers never to take more passengers than the car has seatbelts, but almost every driver would let riders squeeze an extra passenger when the surge was high. Turning away a ride meant arguing with customer service that you deserved a cancellation fee, and every second spent disputing the situation with a company that doesn't care is money that you aren't making, money that you can't afford to do without. It's easier to take the ride, take the risk, and take the money.

. . .

"Did you know your shmeevee taxel is broken?"

I picked my head up from my phone and stared at the oil change technician. He repeated himself.

"Your peevee faxel is busted."

Seeing my confusion, he tried again, speaking slowly.

"On the front right, your CV axle is broken. You've probably been hearing a clicking noise when you hit a bump. It's going to give out soon."

I nodded and mumbled that I knew it was messed up. I had no idea what a CV axle was, but I had been hearing a loud click-bang every time I exited a parking lot for several months. I'd ignored it because I feared what it would mean, but with the knowledge that something really was broken, I had to have it checked out. The last thing I wanted was to break down in the middle of a ride or during one of my days with Alex. I left and headed for a nearby mechanic that I had used before. I had no idea what something like this would cost, but I couldn't risk having my axles fail and drop my entire front end onto the pavement while I was driving.

The mechanic had no good news for me. That I'd been able to drive so far without having a major breakdown was classified as a miracle, because it wasn't just the right axle that was busted. The left axle was also about to give way, and on any given bump in the road, there was a chance that either one of them could fail. I needed the car badly, but the repairs would cost thousands of dollars, more than the car was actually worth, especially with as many miles as I had been putting on it. In just a few years, I'd pushed my car well past the hundred-thousand-mile mark, and there was no end in sight.

Buying a new car wasn't an option, nor was trading in for a used one. My budget was stretched tight as it was. There was no way I could afford a car payment, and I needed a car that the apps would accept. Uber and Lyft both required that a driver's vehicle be a newer model, and although the standards weren't very high, I couldn't just buy an old junker and start picking up rides in it. I didn't just need a car, I needed *this* car, but *this* car needed several thousand dollars to be safe to drive.

Maybe there was a better decision to be made, to trade this car for a used vehicle that barely fit the requirements. I probably could have saved money in the long run by getting rid of an aging vehicle with a zillion miles in stop-and-go traffic, but that required dealing with too many unknowns. Could I find a car? Would it be affordable? Could I make the payments? What if my vehicle broke down in the meantime? I had to pick from a bevy of bad options.

One oft-cited figure from the US Federal Reserve is that 40 percent of US households would struggle to pay a single emergency expense of just $400.[1] Like so many other people struggling to get by, I had to hold my nose and pick the solution that solved the immediate problem, not the long-term one. I pulled the only credit card that had any room left on it out of my wallet and told the mechanic to get me back on the road. It was a solution that hurt because I knew it was irresponsible. I had saved up an emergency fund because I knew I was one major expense away from disaster, but the little that I had been able to save by working my car and my body wasn't enough. It didn't matter that I had worked myself to exhaustion and bled myself dry to have money for a rainy day. The rain had come and flooded away my hopes anyway.

There was one chance that I could make a dent in the cost of the repairs: Halloween. For some reason, Halloween week was the single most profitable time of year. People came from as far as Miami to party with the students, and the festivities lasted for the entire week. It was a raucous, bizarre week where the map would burn with surge pricing the entire time. The rides would come one after another, with no breaks. The only limit to how much money I could make was what my body could stand. Just a few weeks away, it was my last, best chance at salvation.

I picked my newly repaired car up from the mechanic on the Monday of Halloween week. The difference in the feel of the vehicle was drastic. Gone was the loud banging when I pulled out onto the road from a parking lot. Gone was the drastic dipping of the front whenever I had to go over a speed bump. The car was fixed, but now I would have to pay for the repairs in sweat and blood.

The calendar was my ally. Halloween fell on a Wednesday that year, and that meant the students would party hard on Wednesday, recover on Thursday, and go out again on Friday and Saturday. I knew their plans from eavesdropping the previous week. In addition, there would be revelers from out of town, and the weather was going to be clear and crisp, not cold enough to discourage going out but just frosty enough for students to call rides rather than walk short distances. It was perfect.

When I left the office on Wednesday, I was already prepared. I had packed a thermos of coffee in the morning, along with snacks and a sandwich for dinner. The car had been fueled and cleaned. I changed clothes in the bathroom at work, walked to the parking lot, and began to drive.

The next few hours passed in a blur. Demand was so high I would be pinged for my next ride mere seconds after I started the current one. Riders were willing to wait upward of half an hour for their driver to arrive, and the map burned a with surge that more than tripled my earnings on each ride. By the time I finally gave in to the demands of my bladder and stopped for a break, I had already earned more than $250. The money that I would have earned in an entire week had been earned in a few hectic hours. With the plan in motion, I forced myself to take a break and reflect on what I had seen.

The students were the same as ever, but everything about them was turned up to a fever pitch. A group of frat boys popped capsules of smelling salts in my backseat and discussed how huffing them was cheaper than cocaine. Girls dressed in all manner of costumes touched up their makeup and left body glitter on my seats. A girl in a miniature pink cowboy hat opened her purse for lip gloss and showed off that it was also filled with take-out condiment containers filled with shots in case her friends ran out of money at the bar.

The roads were clogged with other drivers, cars covered in company stickers and light-up signs that helped passengers to identify them. Over time, I had come to identify many of the other drivers on the road. We were circling the same area every weekend for hours at a time, and it was inevitable that we would begin to recognize each other. By nodding at each other during pickups and stopping for short snippets of conversation in parking lots, we shared our trials and tribulations. We were all trying to make our way by working the same area. In lean times, any ride that we took was one less for the competition. On busy nights, we waved and smiled as we raked in our earnings. We were simultaneously competitors and comrades, all dancing to the same algorithmic song.

The costumes varied widely in quality, with groups of students opting for lazy choices like "sexy construction worker" (shirtless despite the low temperatures), "girl in corset," and a large number of sexy nurses that made me wonder if they had any idea what actual nurses spent their time doing. Other students sported elaborate outfits, including a ship's captain and a highly detailed Willy Wonka. One student wore an elaborate cactus getup that defied expectations by being ruthlessly unsexy. Among these students were hordes in adult-size onesies that turned them into Care Bears and Pokémon. The only commonality to the crowds was their fierce desire to move from party to party.

When I finally returned to my apartment, I was jittery from caffeine and stiff from sitting in the driver's seat for hours on end. I had only stopped because I needed to sleep before going to work the next day. On the app, the map burned with the promise of more money, if only I would log back on. I wanted nothing more than to stay out, to pay off the repairs, but no single night of work was going to pay off the thousands of dollars I owed now. It would be important to pace myself.

Leaving work on Friday, I took my time to prepare myself physically for what was about to happen. What I had seen on Wednesday would repeat itself, and I had to be ready to put in the hours that would be necessary. I planned to stay out as long as I could, and that would mean late-night fast food, forcing myself to take breaks, and ingesting enough caffeine to make my heart flutter. I knew where I needed to be, how to take care of myself, and how to work the crowds. All that remained was to put in the hours.

Nine hours later, the bars closed. I was stiff, exhausted, and shaky from forcing myself awake with gas station sodas and energy drinks. When I sat still, my heart pounded in my chest even as my eyes drooped. My head felt thick on my shoulders, and my ankle ached from the constant flex of putting my foot on the gas and brake pedals. The money had been tremendous, over $600 in a single night with the promise of more the next day. It was nowhere near what I needed to pay off the axles but enough to put a major dent in the bill. I hoped I'd be able to make the rest of the money in the coming weeks by working extra hours and returning to plasma donation.

I picked up a few more rides, but my body was giving out. I needed badly to rest, to sleep and let my body decaffeinate itself. As the clock neared 3 a.m., I picked up one final ride near a night-club in a strip mall. The students in the backseat were quiet, spent from drinking and dancing. As I dropped them off, they mumbled their thanks and stumbled toward their dorm. I logged off, ready to head home. I took a moment to rub my eyes and think about how I had to do it all again the next day.

I turned away from the college, making my way to the street that would lead me back to my apartment. In the distance, blue lights strobed in the night. Traffic slowed to one lane, and I took a moment to examine the chaos. Two cars had collided in an intersection, the force of one pushing the other off the road and into a large oak tree. The car in the street was a mangled wreck, with broken glass and pieces of the frame littering the roadway. The car against the tree looked much the same, but with one major difference. In its back window was the same black and silver Uber sticker that adorned my windows.

I didn't recognize the car, but that didn't stop me from worrying about its driver. The violence of the collision had surely injured someone, but there was no sign of the vehicles' owners. Perhaps they had already been carted away in an ambulance, which I had been unable to afford when it was my turn to face disaster. The intersection was one that had always worried me, and this wasn't the first accident I had seen there. Most of the time, I was able to tell myself that I was a good driver, that I was far too careful to cause a wreck, but this delusion hid the obvious truth: any accident would ruin me, even if it wasn't my fault. There was no safety net to catch me if I fell, and every night, I forced myself to go back out on the tightrope, all so that I could earn the privilege of making it through one more week.

I shivered, wanting suddenly to be home as I crunched across the broken glass of the intersection. We were all desperate, so we took the next ride, pushing ourselves to do another and another, always whispering quiet prayers that if something were to happen, let it not happen to us. We pushed ourselves to the breaking point and beyond, hoping that we would make it home rather than be the ones that ended up against the tree in a mound of broken glass and shattered plastic.

## CHAPTER 10

I EMERGED FROM HALLOWEEN WEEKEND WITH ENOUGH MONEY TO PAY FOR half the repairs and a burning desire to find a real human connection. Knowing that I could save up money with extra work and plasma donation, I made plans to take Alex to Alabama for Thanksgiving to visit my parents. In the early weeks of November, I put in extra hours behind the wheel and made two visits a week to the plasma center. If I was going to go out of town, I had to make the money I would be missing out on ahead of time. The week of Thanksgiving wasn't known for being busy for rideshare, and I told myself that I wasn't really missing out on much. Besides, my parents deserved to have more time with their grandchild, and I relished the chance to take a few days away from driving. The four days we would be gone would be the longest stretch I had gone without gig work in years.

Visiting my childhood home also meant having to face the inevitable barrage of awkward questions that I could avoid in phone calls. For as many questions as I'd faced from my passengers, I was always able to change the subject or lie. With my parents, that wasn't going to be an option. I wasn't sure if I would be able to bear telling them the reality of what my life had been over the past two years. They knew that I was working two jobs, but I had

made it sound like an occasional thing. Nights and weekends
just to make a little extra, because I couldn't admit that I hadn't
had an actual weekend for nearly three years. The truth that I
was spending every waking moment working just to avoid living
in my car would have been inconceivable and deeply shameful.

Nana and Pop Pop (as Alex called them) greeted us in the
driveway. The dogs ran around us as I unpacked the car and Alex
ran to hug his grandparents. Amid greetings and barking dogs,
there was a sense of relief that washed over me. To spend the
week of Thanksgiving away from Tallahassee was a treat. Leaving
behind the world of apps and rides was a chance to have a sense
of normalcy, a chance to live the sort of life that I yearned for,
one free of the ever-present ghosts of scarcity and precarity. For
a few blessed days, I could give Alex everything that he deserved
and the full attention of a father who loved him more than anything else.

To take these few days off felt like a ridiculous luxury, and I
forced myself to push away the guilt that came with turning off
the apps and having a real life. I deserved a moment's peace. My
son deserved to see his grandparents, and I deserved to rest. Every
part of my psyche resisted. I had been trained, both overtly by
my circumstances and implicitly by the apps, to treat every moment away from the wheel as lost earnings, a missed opportunity
to hustle my way to success. Even as we arrived at the house, I
couldn't help but open up the Uber Driver app to see whether I
was eligible to drive in Alabama. Maybe once Alex was asleep,
the app whispered, you could make a little extra. I shoved my
phone in my pocket and went to greet my family.

The house was a wonderland of small luxuries that I had forgotten about. There was central heat, not a wall-mounted unit.

There was a kitchen with more space in one cabinet than in my entire pantry. There was a garage to park in and a shower with enough hot water to let you really, truly be clean. My mother had laughed as I carried in the bags from the car when she saw that I'd brought my laundry, but I wasn't going to miss a chance to do that chore for free instead of paying for the privilege.

During the days, Alex exhausted himself exploring parks and playing with the dogs, and my parents doted on him relentlessly. When he inevitably crashed into bed, it gave ample time for me to sit and reconnect with my family. On the comfy couch in the living room, we chatted during the commercial breaks of TV shows, my parents muting the television so that we could talk.

Our conversations started on the simplest of subjects and slowly became more and more in depth. Curiosity abounded about my work, Alex's school, and whether I was dating anyone. I had become used to sharing pieces of myself with passengers, but there was something especially difficult about discussing my situation with my parents. Even though they lived a state away and had no ability to affect my day-to-day life, I wanted desperately to smooth over the rough edges, to pretend that everything was just fine.

Yes, I said, my apartment was working out great. The trains reminded me of living in Chicago, and I hardly noticed them anymore. My job was going well, and yes, I had put on some weight but was planning to get back to working out any day now. All of the questions were easily deflected until we came to the thing that interested them the most, that funny taxi-driving thing I was doing on the weekends.

The questions started with the basics. How did it work? Did Uber pay for my gas? How was my car holding up? Was I putting a lot of miles on it? These I was able to answer honestly, but as the days moved on, the subject came up again and again. Each night, the questions became more detailed.

A few days into our visit, my parents had become accustomed to my exhausted demeanor, and they no longer questioned why I reveled in the ability to take a nap during the daytime while they entertained Alex. At night, I told them the more interesting stories from my time on the road, careful to always exclude the most upsetting details. Work was fine, Alex was thriving, and I was getting by. I could not bear to tell them the reality: I could survive but not thrive. It was an ugly truth. I had made my peace with it, but I knew they would struggle to understand.

How much I was driving was a question that I breezed past as best I could, insisting that it was just nights and weekends here and there, a little extra just to make ends meet. I couldn't bring myself to describe the long nights and endless shifts of driving until my body ached and my eyelids drooped. I described passengers as mostly quiet and polite rather than the seedier reality, and I didn't breathe a word about being assaulted. These answers seemed to satisfy their curiosity.

On the day before our departure, there was a visit to the local zoo. Somewhere between the elephant exhibit and the tigers, I noticed how intently my parents were watching not just Alex but me. As we walked from one area to another, their eyes shifted constantly between Alex's childlike awe and my dogged determination to keep him close. They strolled behind us, keeping us both in view.

That night, after Alex had fallen asleep, my father sat down with me in the kitchen. Both he and my mother were concerned. I seemed tired. He asked again about my gig work. Was I actually making any money? I told him that I was, that it was paying my bills, and things would probably be better in the future.

"You're making a lot of sacrifices," he told me.

I shifted uncomfortably and tugged at the arms of my shirt. I had chosen my wardrobe carefully before the trip so that the sleeves would be long enough to cover the obvious needle marks in my elbows from donating plasma. Months of donations had left divots in each arm. Had they noticed? Did they know?

I said that my days were long, but I was doing my best. I said that I had found a way to live simply, and I was finding peace in simplicity because it let me focus on what mattered. My father asked if I was saving for retirement, a question that seemed so detached from my daily reality that I struggled not to burst out laughing. The idea of a day when I could stop working felt fantastical, like being asked if I was going to get home by sprouting wings and flying away. I brushed the question off by referencing a pension plan for state workers. Most employees thought the plan would be killed off some time in the near future in favor of 401(k) plans, but I left that part out.

He asked what I thought about Alex's development, how he'd handled life after the divorce. In one great tide, all of my fears poured out of me. I worried that I would never be able to give him very much, that I was absent from the moments that really mattered. I worried that I had somehow destroyed his chances before he would ever know them. I worried that I wasn't enough for him, that I was doing a bad job of being a real father.

"Don't think like that," he interrupted gently. "I've seen the way you act with him. You watch over him like he's the most precious thing in the world. He'll have his own challenges, and that's what you'll be there to help him with. That's the thing about being a parent. You do everything the best you can, and no matter how well you do, you always feel like you did it wrong."

I could see in his eyes the heavy weight of his own judgment upon himself. All of the guilt I felt at my situation was mirrored in his worry about how his son was faring. Everything he and my mother had done for me, and here I was, barely scraping by. Had he failed? Had I? Guilt, shame, and regret swirled around us in equal measures.

"I see your sacrifices," he said finally. "Someday, he will too."

He slid a check for $200 across the table. For gas money, he said, although we both knew it was far more than that. Maybe I could take some time off from driving and do some things for myself? Use it to get home and plan something special for Alex. Christmas was coming, after all. I thanked him and tucked the check in my pocket. Tomorrow, we would start the journey back to Tallahassee, and I would go back to the grim reality that was my everyday life.

As our visit came to a close, Alex was anxious and restless. We returned from Thanksgiving on Saturday, beating the crowds on the road by coming home a day early. It gave Alex a chance to return to the pace of a regular day with Marie before being thrown back into the stress of school. The drive home was long and particularly boring for a hyperactive child confined to the backseat of a car. Though I tried to break the journey up with stops and singalongs, books and games, there was no hiding his disappointment at leaving Alabama.

His was not the only heart that struggled with the return journey. Coming back to Tallahassee meant returning to the tiny world that I had created for myself, one populated with late nights and backseat strangers.

Our arrival was late, driven by a lunch that my parents in-sisted on buying for us before we left as well as a series of highway accidents that slowed our travel to a crawl. I had planned for us to return in the afternoon, to give Alex time to have dinner with Marie before bedtime. With the delays, we arrived after dark. Marie greeted us at the door and helped put away Alex's bag, plug in the nightlight, and hook up the sound machine that were the essential elements of his bedtime environment. As I car-ried a stuffed tiger and a favorite pillow back to Alex's room, he chattered endlessly with his mother about all the fun of the trip.

Without the need for discussion, Marie and I both knew that I would put him to bed. There were still places where we clashed and struggled to see eye to eye, but our instincts for Alex were closely aligned. I grabbed his pajamas and drew a bath while Alex described a trampoline park he had visited with my parents. Once he was clean and dressed, he hugged Marie goodnight and dutifully headed to his room for our bedtime routine.

For years, Alex and I had ended every night by reading to-gether. His verbal abilities had always been far ahead of his other skills, and Marie and I both enjoyed challenging him by reading books that would have stymied other children. From an early age, Alex was bored by the books that most children enjoyed, and we had been forced to look for more mature titles. For months, we had been slowly working our way through a children's version of *Moby Dick*, something I had sworn I would read to him even before he was born.

We had saved the final chapters for our return, and Alex sat enraptured as I read him the final moments of the *Pequod*. When Ahab and the white whale slipped below the waters, he mumbled sleepily that he'd known that they'd never catch that whale. I finished the last chapter and put the book away on his bookshelf, explaining to him that the whale was a symbol of a thing that can never be attained, yet Ahab looked for it anyway. As I tucked him in, he surprised me suddenly by sitting up and throwing his arms around me.

"I love you, Dad," he whispered to me, a rare unprompted display of affection. I hugged him back with all my might, wishing that I could hold him forever in that moment. We stayed like that for a long time, each of us unwilling to let go and end our time together. When we finally relented, I looked down at him and blinked away the tears that had come while we had squeezed each other. I pulled up his blankets and rumpled his hair before giving him a kiss and reminding him to be good to his mother the next day.

Making my way out of the house, my phone buzzed in my pocket. Without looking, I already knew what it said. Because I had been offline for several days, the apps were now trying to lure me back online. As I climbed back into my car, I set the phone in my dashboard mount and swiped away the notification telling me that drivers in my area were earning big money on Saturday night.

I sat in the darkness for a long time as I pondered what to do with myself. I'd already been on the road for hours. My body ached and I wanted nothing more than a shower and a good night's rest. Still, there was something that had to be done. I opened up the driver apps and logged on.

As I made my way to my first pickup of the night, I thought about the little boy in that house, tucked in under a weighted blanket and dreaming with all the hope that a child's mind can produce. What he wanted from life was so simple for him yet so complex for us. His desires for now were small, and I said a silent prayer that my ability to provide for him would grow at the same pace as his dreams.

I did not know who my passenger would be or what the night would bring, just as I did not know what the future would bring for us. Instead, I moved forward step by step, at every moment making the best decisions that I could. I could not promise him that I would be able to give him the world, but I knew that within me was the ability to push forward no matter what.

For him, I could do anything.

.  .  .

Improving my situation wasn't something that came quickly. Years of grinding away at two jobs took its toll on my mental and physical health, but it did eventually begin to bear fruit. Two serendipitous events gave me the break I needed.

At work, I received an unexpected surprise: I was selected for a promotion. Over the past year, I had closed nearly a dozen cold cases, ranging from car accidents to suicides to a handful of homicides. The identification of these remains gave closure to the families and allowed local agencies to close out cases that had sat unattended for decades. In recognition for my efforts, I was being nominated for advancement to the next tier of the analyst progression.

To be selected for promotion was unexpected. When I first arrived at my position, I had already qualified for a raise under a progression plan for intelligence analysts, but my boss made it clear that there was zero chance that I would be put forward for advancement. This was not an act of malice on her part but a frank assessment of my situation. Given the way that I had been thrust upon her, there was no way to justify promoting me.

Somehow, I had overcome the stench of failure that had clung to me from my old position.

The promotion came with a change in title and a nearly 20 percent raise. The change took a bit to go through, but my spirits were lifted by the knowledge that fate had finally seen fit to give me some breathing room. As I waited for the people above me to sign off on my new position, I daydreamed that my new salary would give me the resources to stop driving, to stay home. I could spend my weeknights relaxing. I could finally find the time to meet people somewhere besides my backseat, to make friends, and maybe even to try my luck dating again. I could already taste my imagined freedom. For months, I'd continued driving at a brutal pace. Working so hard had allowed me to pay off a little bit of my debts each month, but there was still plenty to go, and the road to freedom was fraught with dangers.

The first paycheck brought me back to reality. The idea that I would be able to stop driving had always been a pipe dream, but seeing the actual numbers ended that fantasy. Debt had removed my ability to make progress, and I certainly wasn't alone in that. Most Americans are badly mired in debts of some form, spending 9.5 percent of their income on debt payments.[1] The average credit card debt in America is a little over $5,200, and I was certainly beyond that even before the axles of my car gave out.[2] There would be no end to driving, no increased ability to save money. The only real improvement in my well-being was the ability to take one night off each week.

I resigned myself to this existence, to one defined not by my personality or my skills but by the sheer number of hours I worked. I would have to exist somewhere in the margins of a real life, as an outsider to those who were able to live a more complete existence. I worked my day job, drove my car, and did my best to be a father. I paid my bills with my salary and my rent with my car. I bought my groceries in cash that came from opening up my veins. Week by week, day by day, I made it work, and I counted myself lucky to do so.

My second bit of fortune came from the internet. I had long considered myself to be undesirable, yet somehow a woman I met online thought differently. I was open about my situation and the complexities of my life, but she saw past my limitations. Within a few short months, we were discussing living together, and a little more than a year after we first met, we moved to a new, bigger apartment away from the train tracks.

I continued to drive on many nights, but splitting expenses let me put the rest of the money I earned toward digging my way out of the hole I'd been in. Combined with the raise, having another person to help with costs let me make real progress. With every debt that was paid down, I was able to move more quickly toward paying down the next one, and finally, there came a day when she sat me down and asked me whether I needed to work so much. She knew that driving carried an inherent risk, and she didn't know what she would do if something happened to me. Her concern resonated, for I no longer wanted a life without her.

I cut back and spent more nights at home. My visits to the plasma center stopped. When I tallied up my total donations, I discovered I had donated a little more than thirty-nine gallons of plasma to make ends meet. No more. I filled my evenings with her and with all the things that I'd neglected for myself. Years after I truly needed it, I took the break for which my battered soul had yearned. I taught myself to paint landscapes by watching old Bob Ross videos on YouTube, watched TV shows I'd only known about from talking to passengers, and worked on the very book you now hold in your hands.

My experience in the gig economy wasn't an experiment. I was not a tourist or a journalist conducting a social experiment. I did not have a safety net to fall back on or a job that I could return to. This was not a temporary assignment or an attempt to "slum it" for a few months to gain some deeper understanding of poverty. This was my life. If, when you read this, you think that I could have done things differently, know that I have no doubt that I made mistakes and could have made better choices. I did the best I could with the resources at my disposal. It is the same calculation that millions of people make every day.

There may be a temptation to think that my story is unusual, a unique tale of woe. As I have lived and worked among the American underclass created by the gig economy, I have found that every driver has stories like mine. Every gig worker and driver and Dasher has had bizarre and dangerous encounters with customers. Every one of us has made ugly sacrifices when the money simply wasn't there. Gig workers place their life, well-being, and mental health on the line for the sake of a few dollars. My experiences were not an exception.

I had a number of advantages as I drove through those long nights. My day job provided me with health insurance and coverage for doctor visits. I had a salaried job that provided me with a steady income outside of my driving (even if it wasn't enough to make ends meet). As vulnerable as I was, I had more stability than the average gig worker. I was only unusual because I had opportunities that other drivers did not. I entered the gig economy with more flexibility and resources than others, but I was still beaten down and broken by it. Imagine how the situation would have unfolded if I had been a single mother or an immigrant or anyone who relies on gig work for their entire income.

As narrow as the tightrope was that I walked, there are other people in even more perilous circumstances. The internet abounds with stories of rideshare drivers and gig workers who are homeless, sleeping in their cars, or living in even more desperate circumstances. Each of these people turned to gig work out of a combination of desperation and ambition, a belief that they could make it work in order to make a better life. They should not be blamed for falling for the lies that were created by neuroscientists and peddled to them with slick, highly misleading advertisements. The system that abused me did the same thing to them. Often, what others have endured was worse than my experience. Gig workers have been beaten, robbed, raped, and murdered all across the world, and the companies that recruit them are allowed to walk away without repercussions. I count myself lucky.

I think I was willing to put up with this sort of abuse because I thought I deserved it. Broken down from my divorce, I started my life in rideshare with very little. I had failed to be a good husband, and I carried the deep shame over that failure with me into my car. My passengers came to be my therapy, but I still needed years to overcome my self-loathing. Over time, I rebuilt myself to something resembling a whole person, but the years of my life spent grinding endlessly behind the wheel are time that is simply gone. There is no great moral lesson to be taken from my experiences. Sometimes suffering is just suffering, arbitrary and without meaning.

In my memories from driving, there are things that stand out. There are the passengers that I've told you about, the strange and wonderful cornucopia of humanity that I encountered every time

I turned on the apps. For every story I've recorded here, know that there are a dozen more that I could have chosen. There are moments of shame and sadness, of wrenching loneliness when I cried bitter tears for the life that I was living.

In moments of reflection, I cannot help but wonder how my son will remember these years. In his youth, will he remember a father who built puzzles and took him on pretend adventures? Will he think of the moments where we laughed and played, or will he remember an exhausted man who was too tired to be fully present? I don't know the answer, but I hope that someday he will be able to see the ways that I sacrificed for him. Even if he cannot, perhaps he will be able to understand why we had so little and forgive me for my failings.

These days, I am still driving, though much less. My taxi duties are limited to a few Fridays each month. I have become a minor internet celebrity from the Twitter account where I began cataloging my rides. This, combined with a few viral threads and convenient retweets from celebrities, gave me an audience that supported me when I decided to give writing a try. I look forward to the day when I can finally delete the driver apps from my phone. I don't think it's very far away.

Alex has blossomed into an incredible child. Diagnoses of autism and ADHD have been a challenge, but we are facing them together. His teachers speak highly of his mind, and he spends his days with me laughing and playing. We take frequent trips to Alabama to visit Nana and Pop Pop. We've made our way from a one-bedroom apartment by the tracks to a small townhouse with a room for Alex to call his own during sleepovers. I still read to him every night we are together.

It's been quite a ride.

# EPILOGUE

MY VULNERABILITY WAS PERSONAL, BUT IT WASN'T UNIQUE. MILLIONS OF PEOPLE in America live in precarious circumstances, working paycheck to paycheck and praying that they can avoid disaster long enough to prepare for the next bill or breakdown. Wage stagnation has hamstrung the American worker so badly that it is no longer enough to work forty hours per week, and those who cannot find the time to work even more hours simply do without. For most Americans, the idea of a vacation is a fantasy, for they work a job that underpays them and guarantees very little. Retirement is a laughable impossibility.

Meanwhile, there is *nowhere* in America where a person working full-time for minimum wage can afford a two-bedroom apartment. Even a one-bedroom is out of reach for 95 percent of renters. To afford an apartment at minimum wage in America would require working seventy-nine hours per week, and that's before adding in small trifles like, say, food.[1]

All of this happened while productivity exploded. Between 1973 and 2013, workers became 75 percent more productive but saw their wages rise only 9 percent. Low-wage workers fared even worse, seeing their income *fall* 5 percent over the same period.[2] The American worker has been slowly conditioned to accept less and less despite creating ever more wealth for companies and the people who run them. Like a frog in boiling water, Americans have seen their opportunities slowly disappear as they succumbed to a voracious cycle of exploitation that has left them in ever more precarious conditions.

The hustle culture that whispers promises of success if only you will work a little bit harder has a dark underside, because to stop working is to waste a chance to earn money. The gig economy markets to these people, the ones who are living a few chewed-up fingernails away from the edge. That is to say, the vast majority of us.

People are what make the gig economy work. Actual human beings are the ones required to drive cars and deliver groceries and pick up takeout, and despite the best efforts of companies to experiment with technology to eliminate them, nothing so far has managed to replace the necessity of people. For all the talk about innovative technology and disruption and finding high-tech ways to deliver things that consumers want, none of the apps that make up the gig ecosystem would function if there wasn't a steady supply of human capital for them to exploit. The gaping maw of the "sharing economy" has an insatiable appetite for blood, and its history is replete with decisions to burn through just as much humanity as money.

The exploitation of gig workers is about much more than simply underpaying them or skimming money from their efforts. The low pay and long hours necessary to survive doing gig work have been well-documented, but there is more to the evil of app-based work than low pay. Just as the companies are unable to function without constant injections of new cash from investors who are tricked into thinking that the companies can one day be profitable, a steady stream of workers are lured into the gig world with promises that can never be true.

This pattern would not be so disturbing if it was isolated to one area or one model of work. If it was only food-delivery drivers in, say, Toronto who were having a bad time, then the logical response would be to assume that there was something wrong in that specific sector, but it isn't just one area of the gig economy that treats workers badly. Across every platform and in every service, gig workers are manipulated and exploited before being discarded.

This is a business model for gig companies, not a series of growing pains or a defect that will be fixed. Across numerous platforms in different countries and even continents, gig work has maintained its exploitive posture. In terms that the software engineers who created the various platforms might recognize, it is a feature of the work, not a bug. Just as the companies themselves cannot function without constant injections of venture capital, they cannot function without wave after wave of increasingly desperate workers who think they can game a system designed specifically to manipulate them.

Every gig company is guilty of this pattern of exploitation, but for the sake of simplicity, it's worth examining the actions taken by Uber. As the largest and most obvious example of the app-based, gig employer that we mean when we talk about this field, Uber is instructive because the company has invested so much time and energy in securing its position. It is more than a decade old, and there is no reason to think that the company's behavior at this point is anything less than deliberate. The tens of billions of dollars that the company has spent developing itself have shown it what works and what does not, and the company takes great pains to experiment on customers and drivers to find its strategy.

The long, slow march toward that fateful day when I first got behind the wheel started in 2009 with the founding of Uber-Cab, a company that needed nearly a full year to come online in its first major city. Following a beta period during 2010, the app premiered in 2011 in San Francisco. Expansion happened rapidly after that, with San Francisco giving way to New York City, then Chicago, Paris, Toronto, and London. During this period, Uber employed drivers rather than recruiting the general public. They drove nicer cars and were expected to act like professionals. The product that most consumers use today when they call for a ride, UberX, didn't premier until 2012. It featured less stringent vehicle requirements that allowed a broader range of cars to qualify for the service. In 2013, Uber allowed drivers to sign up with their personal vehicles, and the race to the bottom accelerated.

Funding during the early years was scant, but once the venture capital machine took notice of Uber, what had started as a trickle of money became a biblical flood. By the fateful Thanksgiving in 2016 when I gave my first ride, Uber had received more than twelve billion dollars in outside funding, and the money would continue rolling in every year. Investors included heavyweights of Silicon Valley funding like Kleiner Perkins and Menlo Ventures, sovereign wealth funds from Qatar and Saudi Arabia, and Wall Street heavyweights like BlackRock and Goldman Sachs. From coast to coast, money poured into the company that was promising to "disrupt" the taxi industry.

Disruption, in this context, is a Silicon Valley buzzword that alludes to the tendency of tech companies to ignore pesky things like labor laws and regulations in favor of doing whatever they want on the path to establishing their place in the market. Uber was notorious for this behavior, often "stealth launching" in cities long before it had authorization to do so. By the time regulators caught up to the company, the presence of ridesharing in the city was treated as a fait accompli, and even the penalties levied against the company were easily paid out of the endless ocean of investment money.

This is in line with the ethos of Silicon Valley in this era, a time where disruption was treated as the highest value. Facebook founder Mark Zuckerberg's motto of "move fast and break things" was at the heart of every startup, but Uber was especially reckless in the ways it chose to do so. The company's internal culture was notorious, and whistleblowers who left the company reported sexism, criminality, and threats, all in service of the idea that the company would make money someday if it kept growing.

In Europe, Uber's malfeasance extended to deliberately courting politicians and hiding information from regulators. The company developed a "kill switch" that would cut off regional offices from corporate data if authorities showed up. It was activated at least a dozen times across multiple countries.[3] Internal documents that were leaked to a group of newspapers in a 2022 exposé known as "The Uber Files" showed that the company was well aware that it was breaking the law and didn't care. As Uber's head of global communications put it, "Sometimes we have problems because, well, we're just fucking illegal."[4]

Uber has employed similar tactics to gain a foothold in countries all over the world. The pattern is identical to what Uber did in the US and Canada: make outlandish promises of big earnings, convince vulnerable people to sign up, and then pull the rug out from under them by lowering wages and reducing incentives. In areas where car ownership is less prevalent than the United

States, the company leaned hard on programs to lease cars to drivers.

Starting in 2015, Uber recruited more than 12,000 drivers in Kenya with early incentives. Drivers took out loans to purchase vehicles and quit otherwise decent jobs to work in rideshare. What started as a dream opportunity quickly became a nightmare when Uber slashed ride prices by 35 percent in July 2016. The sudden loss of earnings caused protests and strikes among drivers. Uber assuaged driver anger with temporary bonuses and a minimum wage promise, and the company promised that returning drivers would see similar (and possibly even higher) wages to the old days. Just like in other countries, the promise was a lie, and drivers found themselves working more to earn less. Repossessions soared, and drivers were left saddled with loans they couldn't afford to pay back.[5]

The situation was even more exploitive in India. The company entered the Indian market in 2013 paying sky-high wages, amounts that one journalist compared to the salary of a multinational executive.[6] Partnerships with lending companies extended loans to thousands of drivers to allow them to purchase vehicles, a program that cared very little for the ability of borrowers to pay back the loans. As Uber India president Amit Jain told the *Financial Times*, "Our goal is to give out leases and give out cars to as many people as possible."[7] Drivers found themselves in the same pattern of abuse by the company, but in an exploitive twist, some Indian drivers found themselves renting vehicles from transportation companies that paid them a flat daily rate and pocketed the rest of the earnings.[8] By 2018, more than 1.5 million Indians were driving for Uber, its local competitor Ola, and other ridesharing apps. Uber slashed earnings so many times that some drivers, saddled with debt from vehicle loans, reported earning as little as $3 per day.[9]

Across Europe, Uber encouraged confrontations between taxi drivers and gig workers, reveling in protests that allowed them to claim that their drivers were victims. In France in January 2016, Uber organized a protest through a supposedly independent drivers' association and then encouraged drivers to attend. When an Uber vice president raised the issue of violent clashes between taxi drivers and gig workers, Uber CEO Travis Kalanick responded that the company's eventual victory would be worth the price paid by drivers. In his words, "Violence guarantee[s] success." A full year before the Paris protest, Uber's top lobbyist in Europe, Mark MacGann, had already told leadership about "months of cars being burned and drivers being beaten up" in Spain.

For recruitment, Uber targets vulnerable populations who are down on their luck, between steady jobs, or in difficult situations. Uber's promises are consistent: flexible hours, good earnings, and on-demand assistance. In an ad for the 2018 Grammy Awards, Uber paired a Best New Artist nominee with a driver who just happened to also be interested in a career in music. The key, according to the artist? Persistence.[10] Just keep trying, and eventually you'll make it. Uber can be part of making your dreams come true.

Glossy ads and sanitized web pages cannot hide the reality of who is signing up for the platform and what their outcomes look like. A study in 2018 of rideshare drivers and their wages in New York City found that nine out of ten drivers for the platform were immigrants.[11] It estimated that raising the minimum wage for drivers to the equivalent of $15 per hour would boost the wages of 85 percent of them. The study estimated the size of the rideshare driver population to have grown by 180,000 over the past five years. To summarize, drivers in New York City, largely immigrants, were being recruited by the tens of thousands each year to work jobs that offered substandard wages, no benefits, and the assumption of all the risks that come with driving for a living. Immigrants have often found refuge in taxi driving as a low-skill way to provide steady employment upon arrival in a new country, but Uber's targeting of immigrants for its platform is different because it makes all the same promises that a non-gig job would make without the pesky necessity of any of its promises needing to be true.

The pattern is well demonstrated by a profile done by *The Atlantic* in June 2018 of a driver on the opposite coast of the US. The driver in the piece is a young Yemeni immigrant named Sakhr Sharafadin who gave up a job at a pizza place to drive for Caviar and later Uber. At first, the money and flexibility allowed him to work and take classes at a community college. To meet the platform's vehicle requirements, he bought a car, putting him $25,000 in debt. When he developed an eye problem that required surgery to fix, Sharafadin charged the costs of the surgery to a credit card. He gave up going to college and drove twelve-hour shifts to make ends meet even as the value of his car plummeted from the wear and tear of driving. He told *The Atlantic* he estimated that he made about $10 per hour despite living in high-cost California.

Exploitation of workers is not limited strictly to actions taken by the company itself, for Uber will gladly assist drivers in exploiting themselves. Rideshare companies place requirements on what vehicles drivers can have, and these minimum standards sometimes lock aspiring drivers out of the program. For a company that needs the workers themselves to come up with the capital investment for a vehicle, any barrier to participation is a major problem. To solve this, Uber developed ways to get people with bad credit and few options behind the wheel.

One particularly nefarious way involved partnerships with unscrupulous lenders. Uber helped tens of thousands of people secure loans to buy or lease cars through Uber-approved partners. Don't have a car you can use for driving? Credit score too low to get a car from a regular dealership? The company's partners would approve nearly anyone, creating a predatory lending program that gave out loans with eye-wateringly high payments.

The *Financial Times* profiled one driver who used the program to get on the road. Grace Mora's car payment cost her $726 per month. Despite wanting to quit, she continued driving just to make the payment (an attitude that likely thrilled Uber's executives). The company helpfully arranged for her to make the exorbitant payments directly through the Uber app, deducting the car payment from her earnings and giving her a 10 percent discount for making the payments by driving for Uber rather than paying the company directly.[12]

Uber ended their leasing program in 2018 and handed it off to external partners that continue to operate it. In its place, Uber now offers drivers the ability to rent cars from national vehicle chains. One such partnership with Hertz offers liability protection, unlimited miles, and standard maintenance for the vehicle for the suffocating cost of $214 per week.[13] If a driver earned $15 per hour (far above average), they would still have to work fourteen hours before earning their first real dollar. Notably not included in the lease or this calculation: fuel.

That's okay though, because Uber had a program for that too: the Uber Fuel Card. Until 2018, drivers could obtain a card from Uber that would let them pay for fuel purchases against their current or future earnings. If a driver wanted to gas up before going online, the Uber app would display a negative balance until they had earned enough to pay back the gas. After that program was discontinued, Uber began to offer a branded debit card in partnership with GoBank. The card is touted to drivers as a perk meant to be used to purchase gas, car repairs, and auto parts. If a driver overdrafts their account, the card will allow a negative balance of up to $100 before turning off. As the website for the program puts it, "Payments for such overdrafts will be deducted from future deposits" (i.e., Uber earnings).

These examples of exploitation are meant to demonstrate the essential nature of the gig economy. It is not merely a system that exploits workers; it relies on lying to people to convince them to exploit themselves. Gig work is not a streamlining of economic relationships but a technologically enabled engine of human trafficking. There are other, equally destructive lies that the companies have told communities. Uber has variously claimed that its services reduced traffic by removing cars from the road and caused drunk-driving rates to drop. Neither of these claims were true, but by the time research had determined that, the company had moved on to claim other supposed benefits.[14]

Wooed by promises of high wages, flexible hours, and independence, drivers end up working long hours for miserably low pay in conditions that damage their vehicles, bodies, and financial well-being. Uber proudly proclaims that it helps US drivers obtain health insurance, but it merely points to the health exchanges available in each state. No funding is provided to help drivers obtain coverage. Very little safety net exists for workers who are injured on the job, develop health problems, or decide to quit. Until the 2020 coronavirus pandemic relief bill, drivers did not qualify for unemployment benefits if they were forced to stop driving. As "contractors" who were treated like independent business owners, they shouldered all the risks, costs, and burdens yet had no control over any part of the actual operation of the business they were supposedly running.

Other, smaller humiliations are also present. Drivers working long hours are often unable to find healthy options for food, and conversations on online forums often center on what food and snacks can be packed in the car. Drivers will turn to unhealthy fast food and gas station meals when they are far from home. The constant desire to be online for fear of missing out pushes them to look for quick options regardless of the health implications. The situation at night is even worse, with drivers who have been working for hours often unable to find meals or an open bathroom during late hours. Using the restroom is a challenge in some cities at the best of times. Grocery stores sometimes do not view gig workers as customers and refuse access to bathrooms. Many restaurants don't allow drivers doing food deliveries to use the facilities, leaving them to pee in disposable cups and discard them on the side of the road.[15]

All of this is creating the new American underclass, a system of on-demand servants who are summoned when needed and dismissed just as easily. There is a digital sweatshop operating in plain sight on every corner, hidden only by the lock screen of the phones in which it lives. The gig economy targets the weakest and most vulnerable members of society, the ones with the fewest options and the most need for an opportunity that seems like a good deal. It lies again and again to recruit them, uses them until they are broken, and then discards them.

Its very existence weakens the foundation of society by recreating the sort of low-paid, piecemeal work that was a hallmark of industrial exploitation at the turn of the twentieth century. Gone are the sweatshops that paid garment makers by the shirt, replaced with apps that convince workers to exploit themselves for less than minimum wage. The gig economy is eating away at the foundations of American life, subjecting its participants to routine humiliation in the name of consumer convenience even as it unravels labor protections.

It is not unreasonable to ask how long such a situation can continue before it crumbles under its own weight. With every app that is added to the gig ecosystem, the waters of poverty rise a few inches, and thousands more people begin drowning. Those who sit comfortably in the middle class and assure themselves that they are "making it" would do well to ask their next Uber driver or Instacart shopper if they have ever had to sleep in their car or skip a meal just to make ends meet.

Between credit card debts, student loan payments, stagnant wages, rising rents and healthcare costs, and working more and more hours, it's no surprise that rideshare companies like Uber have stepped into the void left by the withering of the American Dream. Many people, myself included, were seduced by the promises of flexibility and freedom, a way to have more by filling the spare moments of our lives with occasional work.

The gig economy ostensibly harnesses this energy by letting people work when and how they would like.[16] It is tailor-made to exploit people with glossy promises of self-empowerment and flexible hours. No longer must a worker balance schedules between two jobs. For the real go-getters, the gig economy offers a buffet of options for earning money when and however you would like. You can deliver food for DoorDash, pick up groceries for Instacart, or do data entry on Amazon's Mechanical Turk. Work your day job, put your kids to sleep, and then earn money completing various tasks on Fiverr. Make a better life, one gig at a time. This magical thinking supposes that nothing will ever go wrong, that everyone can and wants to work endlessly in every waking moment.

The gig economy posits itself as a technological solution to the income gap, a convenient way for people to log on, work for short periods, then get back to living their lives when they need to log off. None of the promotional materials discuss limited opportunities, long nights, and degrading conditions. The focus in every ad for a new app, whether it involves delivering packages or groceries or take-out food, is on how workers can make good money in their spare time doing simple tasks. The apps advertise convenience to consumers and prosperity for the workers, but what they neglect to mention is the inability of any gig worker to have a life outside of the app.

Somehow, gig platforms have all stumbled upon a magic formula for making these sorts of concierge services available to the public at a price that is easy to swallow. The ability to charge these rock-bottom prices is because gig companies are subsidized by billions in venture capital funds. Investors are more than willing to tolerate the incineration of vast sums of money so long as the company goes public in time for them to recoup their losses at the expense of the retail suckers who will invest in a company without understanding how it is able to provide a service at so low a cost. If the stock price eventually plummets and the company falls apart because it can't turn an actual profit? Well, the original investors will be long gone by then, off to invest in the next unicorn that promises to move fast and break things, regardless of whether the things being broken are essential services or people's lives.

There is a convenience factor to the apps and their services, but their activities are hollowing out the space beneath America's shrinking middle class. By eradicating basic worker protections in favor of vulnerable on-demand workers, the entire economy is dragged downward. While not quite gig workers, Amazon warehouse workers provide a good example of the effect. Amazon warehouses churn through tens of thousands of employees each year as they hire and fire for seasonal variations. These warehouse workers are hired through temp agencies and can be fired on a whim, often for minor infractions like "getting sick" or failing to keep up a breakneck pace. In 2014, warehouse workers in Robbinsville, New Jersey, made an average of $24 per hour. After an Amazon warehouse opened in the area, wages plummeted to $17.50 per hour in 2020. Meanwhile, at the grueling Amazon fulfillment centers around the country, workers are told that they should celebrate the decision to raise the minimum wage in their warehouse to $15 per hour.[17] The race to the bottom accelerates as consumers are conditioned to expect instant gratification, but don't worry. Amazon itself has a gig job you can do: delivering packages via Amazon Flex.

There is a cost being paid for these apps to exist, and it's more than the money that's propping up the gig economy. A deeply immoral vein of suffering runs through every enterprise in this new world. The people who give rides and deliver groceries and pick up to-go orders from restaurants are being abused by a system that only functions because it is financed by sovereign wealth funds and venture capital investors. The companies survive by lying to the people doing the actual work and hiding the real costs of their convenience. They squeeze the most vulnerable and desperate members of an already dysfunctional society.

The gig economy promises consumers an endless array of servants to make your life easier, to lift the burden of drudgery from your shoulders. Pull out your phone, tap a few times, and let the app and its magical elves simplify your life. Your food can be left at your door, appearing from thin air so long as you don't bother to think about the desperate sucker who is running all over town chasing the money to pay the rent. Your groceries can be delivered by a single mother whose smiling face masks her vulnerability because she *needs* you to give her a five-star review. And when these workers try to log off, the apps question their leaving, as if work is the default state of human existence. Welcome to the gig economy.

Don't rest. Don't sleep. Don't stop.

# ACKNOWLEDGMENTS

THIS BOOK WOULD NOT HAVE BEEN POSSIBLE WITHOUT THE SUPPORT OF MY friends and family, as well as the goodwill and generosity of so many people who have never met me. To my darling Mysheka, know that your love and support as I tapped away endlessly at my computer meant the world to me. Every word of encouragement, kind touch, and head scratch buoyed my soul as I pushed to bare it upon these pages.

I am indebted to my agent, Max Edwards, for his unwavering belief that this book was possible. When he first reached out to me on Twitter and asked to take a look at the notes I had been jotting down, I had no idea that those notes would become the work that you see in front of you. In those disconnected paragraphs, he saw something was possible, and with time, I came to see it as well.

To the many thousands of people who have followed me on Twitter, who donated to support my writing and left me words of kindness and encouragement, know that this book only exists because of your assistance. From the bottom of my heart, thank you.

Finally, I must give thanks to the friends who stayed with me on this journey. I lost a great deal over the years, but I will always cherish the Heroes for Hire who stayed by my side. Early chapter drafts and outlines were vastly improved by your input.

# NOTES

CHAPTER 2

1. This system of percentage bonuses was later changed to a flat dollar amount bonus on the ride, a system that reduced driver earnings despite assurances by Uber to the contrary.

2. Every story in this book about a rider and their behavior is true. There are no composites or combinations of people used to construct fanciful tales. I have changed the names to protect their privacy (and dignity), but every one of them was a real person who sat in my backseat.

CHAPTER 3

1. Keith Bailey and James Spletzer, "Using Administrative Data, Census Bureau Can Now Track the Rise in Multiple Jobholders," US Census Bureau, February 3, 2021, https://www.census.gov/library/stories/2021/02/new-way-to-measure-how-many-americans-work-more-than-one-job.html.

2. Lydia Saad, "The '40-Hour' Workweek Is Actually Longer—by Seven Hours," Gallup, August 29, 2014, https://news.gallup.com/poll/175286/hour-workweek-actually-longer-seven-hours.aspx.

3. Stacy Weiner, "A Growing Psychiatrist Shortage and an Enormous Demand for Mental Health Services," American Association of Medical Colleges, August 9, 2022, https://www.aamc.org/news-insights/growing-psychiatrist-shortage-enormous-demand-mental-health-services.

CHAPTER 4

1. Jonathan Hall and Alan Krueger, *An Analysis of the Labor Market for Uber's Driver-Partners in the United States*, National Bureau of Economic Research, January 22, 2015, p. 9.

2. Amir Efreti, "How Uber Will Combat Rising Driver Churn," *The Information*, April 20, 2017, https://www.theinformation.com/articles/how-uber-will-combat-rising-driver-churn.

3. Noam Sheiber, "How Uber Uses Psychological Tricks to Push Its Drivers' Buttons," *New York Times*, April 2, 2017, https://www.nytimes.com/interactive/2017/04/02/technology/uber-drivers-psychological-tricks.html.

CHAPTER 5

1. Dear Ophelia, I was later told that somewhere in this mayhem, I shoved you quite hard. If you should ever read this, know that I am very sorry for that. You were in no way to blame for what happened, and it was wrong of me, even in my addled state, to push you.

2. While the names of all other passengers have been changed to protect their privacy, this name has not been changed.

3. Felicity Lawrence and Jon Henley, "'Violence Guarantees Success': How Uber Exploited Taxi Protests," *The Guardian*, July 10, 2022, https://www.theguardian.com/news/2022/jul/10/violence-guarantees-success-how-uber-exploited-taxi-protests.

4. Douglas MacMillan, "Uber Promised South Africans Better Lives but Knew Drivers Risked Debt and Danger," *Washington Post*, July 11, 2022, https://www.washingtonpost.com/business/2022/07/11/uber-driver-south-africa-attacks.

CHAPTER 6

1. Jonathan Hall and Alan Krueger, *An Analysis of the Labor Market for Uber's Driver-Partners in the United States*, National Bureau of Economic Research, January 22, 2015.

2. Matt McFarland, "Uber's Remarkable Growth Could End the Era of Poorly Paid Cab Drivers," *Washington Post*, May 27, 2014, https://www.washingtonpost.com/news/innovations/wp/2014/05/27/ubers-remarkable-growth-could-end-the-era-of-poorly-paid-cab-drivers.

3. Brett Helling, "Ridester's 2018 Independent Driver Earnings Survey," *Ridester* (blog), updated February 24, 2022, https://www.ridester.com/2018-survey.

4. Andrew Johnson, "Uber Agrees to Pay $20 Million to Settle FTC Charges That It Recruited Prospective Drivers with Exaggerated Earnings Claims," Federal Trade Commission, January 19, 2017, https://www.ftc.gov/news-events/news/press-releases/2017/01/uber-agrees-pay-20-million-settle-ftc-charges-it-recruited-prospective-drivers-exaggerated-earnings.

5. *Uber 2021 Proxy Statement*, Uber, https://investor.uber.com/financials/default.aspx.

6. Tina Bellon and Nivedita Balu, "Uber Makes First Operating Profit as Driver Shortage Eases," Reuters, November 4, 2021, https://www.reuters.com/technology/uber-posts-first-small-adjusted-profit-ridership-rises-delivery-gets-more-2021-11-04.

7. Jackie Davalos, "Uber Gains After Posting First Adjusted Profit on Ride Recovery," *Bloomberg*, November 4, 2021, https://www.bloomberg.com/news/articles/2021-11-04/uber-posts-first-profit-on-ride-hailing-rebound-delivery-demand; "Uber Reports First Quarterly Profit as Rides Recover," *Al Jazeera*, November 4, 2021, https://www.aljazeera.com/economy/2021/11/4/uber-reports-quarterly-gains-as-rides-recover.

8. Uber, "Uber Announces Results for Second Quarter 2023," news release, August 1, 2023, https://investor.uber.com/news-events/news/press-release -details/2023/Uber-Announces-Results-for-Second-Quarter-2023/default.aspx.

9. Hubert Horan, "Can Uber Ever Deliver? Part Twenty-Nine: Despite Massive Price Increases Uber Losses Top $31 Billion," *Naked Capitalism* (blog), February 11, 2022, https://www.nakedcapitalism.com/2022/02/hubert -horan-can-uber-ever-deliver-part-twenty-nine-despite-massive-price -increases-uber-losses-top-31-billion.html.

10. Cory Doctorow, "The Big Lie That Keeps the Uber Bezzle Alive," *Medium* (blog), February 11, 2022, https://doctorow.medium.com/the-big -lie-that-keeps-the-uber-bezzle-alive-8d6e8c0ccde7.

11. Hugh Sun, "Uber Co-Founder Travis Kalanick Is on Pace to Sell His Entire Stake in the Ride-Hailing Giant," CNBC, December 22, 2019, https://www.cnbc.com/2019/12/22/uber-co-founder-travis-kalanick-is-on -pace-to-sell-his-entire-stake.html.

12. Annie Palmer, "Travis Kalanick Severs All Ties with Uber, Departing Board and Selling All His Shares," CNBC, December 24, 2019, https:// www.cnbc.com/2019/12/24/travis-kalanick-to-depart-uber-board-of -directors.html.

13. Deirdre Bosa and Ryan Browne, "Uber CEO Tells Staff Company Will Cut Down on Costs, Treat Hiring as a 'Privilege,'" CNBC, May 9, 2022, https://www.cnbc.com/2022/05/09/uber-to-cut-down-on-costs-treat -hiring-as-a-privilege-ceo-email.html.

14. Ethan Baron, "Bay Area's DoorDash to Pay $2.5 Million After Being Accused of Stealing Drivers' Tips," *Mercury News*, November 25, 2020, https://www.mercurynews.com/2020/11/25/bay-areas-doordash-to-pay-2-5 -million-after-being-accused-of-stealing-drivers-tips.

15. Ethan Baron, "Uber, Lyft Would Owe California $413 Million in Unemployment Funds If Drivers Were Considered Employees: Report," *Mercury News*, May 11, 2020, https://www.mercurynews.com/2020/05/11 /uber-lyft-would-owe-california-413-million-in-unemployment-funds-if -drivers-were-considered-employees-report.

16. Shirin Ghaffary, "Uber and Lyft Say They Don't Plan to Reclassify Their Drivers as Employees," *Vox*, September 11, 2019, https://www.vox.com /2019/9/11/20861599/ab-5-uber-lyft-drivers-contractors-reclassify-employees.

17. Kate Conger and Kellen Browning, "A Judge Declared California's Gig Worker Law Unconstitutional. Now What?" *New York Times*, August 23, 2021, https://www.nytimes.com/2021/08/23/technology/california-gig -worker-law-explained.html.

18. Jelisa Castrodale, "California Supermarkets Fire Union Delivery Drivers, Replace Them with Gig Workers as Proposition 22 Takes Effect," *Food and Wine*, January 5, 2021, https://www.foodandwine.com/news /california-supermarkets-fire-union-drivers-prop-22.

CHAPTER 9

1. "Report on the Economic Well-Being of U.S. Households in 2017," Board of Governors of the Federal Reserve System, May 2018, https://www.federalreserve.gov/publications/files/2017-report-economic-well-being-us-households-201805.pdf.

CHAPTER 10

1. Board of Governors of the Federal Reserve System (US), "Household Debt Service Payments as a Percent of Disposable Personal Income [TDSP]," Federal Reserve Bank of St. Louis, January 9, 2023, https://fred.stlouisfed.org/series/TDSP.

2. Lyle Daly, "Average American Credit Card Debt in 2022: $5,221," *The Motley Fool*, June 16, 2022, https://www.fool.com/the-ascent/research/credit-card-debt-statistics.

EPILOGUE

1. "Out of Reach: The High Cost of Housing," National Low Income Housing Coalition, 2020, https://reports.nlihc.org/sites/default/files/oor/OOR_BOOK_2020.pdf.

2. Lawrence Mishel, Elise Gould, and Josh Bivens, "Wage Stagnation in Nine Charts," Economic Policy Institute, January 6, 2015, https://www.epi.org/publication/charting-wage-stagnation.

3. Rob Davies and Simon Goodley, "Uber Bosses Told Staff to Use 'Kill Switch' During Raids to Stop Police Seeing Data," *The Guardian*, July 10, 2022, https://www.theguardian.com/news/2022/jul/10/uber-bosses-told-staff-use-kill-switch-raids-stop-police-seeing-data.

4. Harry Davies, Simon Goodley, Felicity Lawrence, Paul Lewis, and Lisa O'Carroll, "Uber Broke Laws, Duped Police and Secretly Lobbied Governments, Leak Reveals," *The Guardian*, July 11, 2022, https://www.theguardian.com/news/2022/jul/10/uber-files-leak-reveals-global-lobbying-campaign.

5. Amanda Sperber, "Uber Made Big Promises in Kenya. Drivers Say It's Ruined Their Lives," NBC News, November 29, 2020, https://www.nbcnews.com/news/world/uber-made-big-promises-kenya-drivers-say-it-s-ruined-n1247964.

6. Sai Sachin Ravikumar, Aditi Shah, and Aditya Kalra, "As Uber Gears Up for IPO, Many Indian Drivers Talk of Shattered Dreams," Reuters, May 8, 2019, https://www.reuters.com/article/us-uber-ipo-india-drivers/as-uber-gears-up-for-ipo-many-indian-drivers-talk-of-shattered-dreams-idUSKCN1SE0OP.

7. Leslie Hook, "Uber Hitches a Ride with Car Finance Schemes," *Financial Times*, April 11, 2016, https://www.ft.com/content/921289f6-5dd1-11e6-bb77-a121aa8abd95.

8. Madhura Karnik, "Uber in India Is Fundamentally Different from Uber in the West," *Quartz India*, March 27, 2017, https://qz.com/india /926220/uber-in-india-is-fundamentally-different-from-uber-in-the -west.

9. Amanda Erickson, "India's Uber Drivers Went on Strike Because They're Making $3 a Day," *Washington Post*, March 19, 2018, https://www .washingtonpost.com/news/worldviews/wp/2018/03/19/indias-uber-drivers -went-on-strike-today-because-theyre-making-almost-nothing.

10. "Uber TV Spot, 'Khalid's Road to Best New Artist Nominee,'" iSpot.tv, January 28, 2018, https://www.ispot.tv/ad/wJkf/uber-khalids-road -to-best-new-artist-nominee.

11. James A. Parrott and Michael Reich, "An Earnings Standard for New York City's App-Based Drivers: Economic Analysis and Policy Assessment," Center for New York City Affairs, The New School, July 2018, http://www.centernyc.org/an-earnings-standard.

12. Leslie Hook, "Uber Hitches a Ride with Car Finance Schemes," *Financial Times*, August 11, 2016, https://www.ft.com/content/921289f6 -5dd1-11e6-bb77-a121aa8abd95.

13. "Uber Driver Rental Car Program," Hertz, https://www.hertz.com /rentacar/misc/index.jsp?targetPage=uber_landing_page.jsp&LinkType =HZLK.

14. "We found that the deployment of Uber services in a given metropolitan county had no association with the number of subsequent traffic fatalities, whether measured in aggregate or specific to drunk-driving fatalities or fatalities during weekends and holidays," Noli Brazil and David S. Kirk, "Uber and Metropolitan Traffic Fatalities in the United States," *American Journal of Epidemiology* 184, no. 3 (August 1, 2016): 192–98. "Based on a set of fixed-effect panel models estimated using metropolitan statistical area level data, we find that the entrance of [transportation network companies] led to increased road congestion in terms of both intensity (by 0.9%) and duration (by 4.5%), an 8.9% decline in transit ridership and an insignificant change in vehicle ownership," Mi Diao, Hui Kong, and Jinhua Zhao, "Impacts of Transportation Network Companies on Urban Mobility," *Nature Sustainability*, no. 4 (2021): pp. 494–500, https://doi.org/10.1038 /s41893-020-00678-z.

15. Edward Ongweso, "Gig Workers Have Nowhere to Pee," *Vice*, January 31, 2020, https://www.vice.com/en/article/884xyp/gig-workers-have -nowhere-to-pee.

16. Julia Beckheusen, "Women More Likely to Have Multiple Jobs," US Census Bureau, June 28, 2019, https://www.census.gov/library/stories /2019/06/about-thirteen-million-united-states-workers-have-more-than -one-job.html.

17. Matt Day and Spencer Soper, "Amazon Has Turned a Middle-Class Warehouse Career into a McJob," *Bloomberg*, December 17, 2020, https://www.bloomberg.com/news/features/2020-12-17/amazon-amzn-job-pay-rate-leaves-some-warehouse-employees-homeless.